DON'T HIT HIM, HE'S DEAD

JOHN McDONOUGH with PAUL T. OWENS

Celestial Arts
Millbrae, California

Library of Congress Cataloging in Publication Data

McDonough, John, 1916-
    Don't hit him, he's dead.

    1.   Football—Anecdotes, facetiae, satire etc.
I.   Owens, Paul T., joint author.   II.   Title.
GV950.5.M33   796.33'2'0207   78-54478
ISBN 0-89087-219-8

    2   3   4   5   6   7 — 8 4   8 3   8 2   8 1   8 0   7 9   7 8

Introduction

I am glad John has decided to do a book on being an official. It's about time somebody did. But there is no way I can stop myself from yelling whenever I see black and white stripes.

When you're out there on the field and they miss something, you're totally helpless. It's worse than being carried out on a stretcher. No matter how much you yell at them there's nothing you can do. They ought to be taken out and shot at least once every season to let them know how it feels for us to have to deal with them.

You can't blame them entirely though. There's just too many things going on all at once. You can't expect six or seven guys to see everything that twenty-two others are doing. Players today are too big and quick. Officials can be blocked right out of their positions and miss everything.

Maybe the best thing would be to have more officials out there and less players. But even if you had twenty officials and six players, somebody would get away with something, and the officials would miss something. It's just the nature of the game. The game is played by people and judged by them, so there's bound to be mistakes. I understand they get rid of officials who make too many. I like that policy. They'll see more if they know their job is constantly on the line. Every game should have officials waiting on the sidelines, to come into the game whenever one of them makes a mistake.

3

Now, as for John, there is nothing he can do—he can't drink—he can't play golf—On the football field, though, he was one of the few who knew how to have a good time. The game was serious business, and no matter how mad you were because some official didn't see somebody damn near beat you to death, you couldn't get mad at John. You knew, you always knew, that as serious as he acted, deep down he wanted to laugh. It was only a game and that's how he wanted to see it.

People don't realize this, but there's more pressure on officials than there is on players. Every time an official calls something somebody is up in his face yelling. And when he doesn't call anything the yelling is worse. And, who wants to be out there wearing only a striped shirt and a pair of white knickers? No way. Not me. I'd rather be in the front line any day.

Deacon Jones, 1978
10 Time All Pro
Defensive Lineman

In writing this story with John I got to know many of the coaches, players and officials who worked with him while he officiated pro football. All of them remembered ways he had of making the game fun, and how effective he was in keeping the show moving.

When I first met John I asked him what it was like to be down there with all that shoving and pushing and knocking each other around. He told me, "I'd have to write a book to tell you, and that probably couldn't tell it all." Well, here, at least, is the book.

Paul T. Owens

The last chapter of John's life ended on July 10th when he died of cancer. This book, upon which he labored so meticulously and enthusiastically for the past year, was on its way to press. It is not only a story about professional football, but also John's stories of the events that shaped his life and of those many friends, students and athletes whom his love for sports brought him into contact. I am grateful to have shared his life and his love for football. This book is a tribute to his memory, a memorial to his vigorous and meaningful life.

BETH MCDONOUGH

If our purpose is to find the good and rejoice in it, then John McDonough is a winner. If our purpose is to seek the highest sense of fairness and demand it as a rule, then John was a human saint. If our purpose is to find ways to make others cheer for themselves and all the loving existence in life, then John won with life and we are all part of his victory. We are grateful that we knew him. We are blessed that he was a part of our lives.

PAUL OWENS

Eulogy for John McDonough
Santa Ana, California
July 14, 1978

ONE

I am tough. I have to be. For thirty-five years I was a football official, fourteen in professional football. In stadiums filled with a hundred thousand people I took the brunt of the booing for those who really deserved it—the players and the coaches. That's *one* reason I don't smile much.

Fans never gave me standing ovations. The people down on the field weren't rooting for me either. Players screamed that they didn't do what I just saw them do. Coaches always wanted me to watch the *other* team. Some captains wanted me to make the penalty decisions for them. The television people thought the television signals were more important than the signals called by the quarterback. Owners were afraid they might lose the game, and a possible trip to the play-offs, because we didn't see everything on every play.

PASS INTERFERENCE

That's another reason officials don't smile much. All those people are very intense about the calls on the field and in the heat of the moment tend to interpret a smile differently. One of them might think it was a smirk or even worse, a sneer. Such frivolity, as a smile, would indicate the official wasn't taking the game very seriously, and to coaches, owners and trainers, it is deadly serious. After all, it is their livelihood. Occasionally, we smile anyway, but not very often.

Officials are like punching bags. Everybody's punching bag. But that's all right. We can take it. No one likes us and they don't have to. We're used to it—but just let them try playing the game without us.

As referee, I was the captain of the third team on the field, the officials, sometimes called the zebras or jailbirds. I was the one who had to step out into the open all by myself and announce decisions against the home team. I was the one who coordinated television with the running of the game. I was the one responsible for keeping order in one of the world's most exciting and violent sports.

There is only one referee in a game. He is the head official. He conducts the pregame officials' conference. He handles the flip of the coin. He is the one to whom the other officials report fouls. He gives the options to the captains. After they decide, he's the one who gives those funny signals. Since the 1976 season he's been hooked up to a microphone, acting as director of fair play and administrator of retribution.

The referee's position at the beginning of every scrimmage play is back there with the quarterback. From 1960 to 1974 I worked with the best quarterbacks in the country. Like many of them, I might still be there if my knees hadn't started to go, and I hadn't lost some of my speed. I still get up every Sunday wondering how I can change the TV channels so that I can get right up there and walk onto the field and start blowing the whistle again.

On October 16, 1966, Joe Namath was quarterbacking for the New York Jets. He was leading his team against the Houston Oilers and at the same time giving me advice on how I could do a better job for him. I was trying to think of how to get him to stop.

First I told him that I wouldn't help him quarterback if he didn't help me referee but that approach didn't stop him. Finally on a third down and long yardage, Joe lofted a bomb way downfield. One of the defensive backs made a great play. He came right over the top of Joe's intended receiver, hit the ball, and knocked him to the ground. The defender had touched the ball first so there was no call for pass interference.

Joe turned to me and said, "For God's sake, why don't you go down there and call something. They're jumping all over my receivers!"

I said, "You're kicking team's coming in, Joe. See you later."

Houston's offense ran three downs for a total of about five yards and kicked the ball back to the Jets. Television asked for a time-out and I gave it to them. Joe and the Jets took the field and I had a whole minute before the commercial break was over.

I called, "Hey, Joe, come here."

He shuffled over. "Yeah, Big John. What do you want?"

"You see those front four?" I pointed to the Oilers line.

He nodded his head.

"You got any idea how much they weigh?"

He shook his head.

"Well, I'll tell you, they run about 265 each and they got one thing on their mind. You know what that is, Joe?"

"What's that?"

"They're gonna rip your head right off your shoulders. So, on the next four or five plays you'd better protect yourself."

"What do you mean?"

"Every time you throw the ball, Joe, I'm standing right next to you, hollering, 'Don't hit him, he's dead!' So those guys know that you've released the ball and they peel away and don't hit you. But I'm not going to be here for the next four or five plays; I'm gonna run downfield to make sure they don't mess with your receivers."

Joe looked at me, then he looked downfield. "You stay right here," he said, "The hell with the receivers." We never had any problems for the rest of the afternoon.

Millions of people watch football every week and I'll bet not one of them thinks anything about what is going on between the officials and the team captains during the coin flip and pregame conference. The coin flip is something that has to be done, and it is done properly among the officials and the captains. And, rightly so. But sometimes that's not all that is going on down there.

The Oakland Raiders were playing the San Diego Chargers

in San Diego (October 21, 1973). I was in the center of the field for the pregame with the captains, Deacon Jones of the Chargers and Gene Upshaw of the Raiders. I have one coin I use for flips. It is a Mexican five peso piece with a picture of Hidalgo inscribed on it. Hidalgo doesn't have a hair on his head. I showed the coin to both of them.

Deacon said as he looked it over, "Let me take a look at this coin. How come you use this? Why don't you use a United States coin?"

"Because I happen to like this one."

"No wonder you like it. It has your picture on it, Baldy."

I took the coin from his hand and asked Gene to call it while it was in the air. He called it "heads" and it came up heads.

I said, "You won, Gene, what do you want to do?"

"We want to receive down there." He pointed.

"That's two choices. You only get one," I told him.

"O. K., we'll receive, but we still want it down there."

"That's still two choices, Gene. I'll take the first one, so your team will receive." I turned to Deacon and told him, "He wants to receive. What are you going to do?"

"I am going to whip his ass all over this field."

All of us started laughing so hard I had to ask my umpire, who was standing there recording the toss on his game card, who had won the toss. Finally I said, "All right, Deacon, he wants the ball. Which end are you going to kick it from?"

"Well, we're very accommodating down here in San Diego. If he wants to receive it down there then we'll kick it to him down there, but I am still going to whip his ass all over this field."

While the people in the stands were sitting down spilling cokes and dripping mustard waiting for the entertainment to start we were already getting our second laugh.

The coin flip used to take place a half hour before kickoff. Now, possibly due to television coverage, it is done about three minutes before game time. I don't know if the rule has been changed concerning flipping during inclement weather, but the referee once had the option of having the flipping ceremonies done in the locker room if the weather was too brutal out in the field area.

On December 22, 1963, I was working in Kansas City. It was six degrees below zero before the game and twelve below when it ended. I don't know about you, but to me six below is definitely inclement weather. I got coaches Hank Stram of Kansas City and Weeb Eubank of the New York Jets together in the dressing room hallway for the flip.

Weeb won the toss and said, "We'll take the ball."

I turned to Coach Stram and he said, "We'll kick it from the scoreboard end."

Weeb then kidded, "Hey, tell your guys to keep their flags in their pockets. This is a nothing game. The championships have already been decided so no one here's going anywhere. We just have to get the game into the book. So, let's get it over with."

I laughed, "Well, tell your guys not to foul and we won't throw any flags. That goes for your team, too, coach," I turned and nodded to Coach Stram.

Before we left the dressing room coin flip area, one of the coaches suggested that the officials should blow a quick whistle because the field was frozen as hard as the street and someone might get hurt bad. I reminded them that the ball carrier could cry "down," and by rule, we would blow the whistle.

They must have told their players that because all afternoon we were blowing our whistles to rescue some ball carrier who was yelling, "down." On one play, the Chiefs' linebacker was holding a scrambling runner off the ground and said to him, "Say 'down,' stupid." The kid screamed, "down," and I blew the play dead.

Once, much to my embarrassment, I found myself working for, rather than with, Bob Griese, Miami's great quarterback. It was in the Houston Astrodome on Sunday, September 27, 1970, and Bob was backed up into his own end zone during the fourth quarter. As he turned to run he was naked, which, in football parlance, means he didn't have anyone to block for him. He was looking for help, and there it was, unfortunately, me.

I started backpedaling as fast as I could go. When I cut right, he cut left. Then I cut left and he cut right. On the third cut, I wiped out both guards of the Houston Oilers. I did a complete back flip, lost my hat and game card. I ended up on my knees watching Griese, still on his feet and running like hell down the sidelines.

I put myself back together and took out after him, hoping someone had called something. I sure didn't want him to make a big gain after all of the blocking I had done for him. He made it to the fifty yard line and when I came flying by even Wally Lemm, the Houston coach, was laughing at me. "They got you that time, didn't they, Baldy?"

When I ran back to get my hat and card, I got a lot of good-natured hooting from the stands. They were booing and laughing at the same time.

When the game was over and we went in to take our showers, I was hurting all over. When I came out I heard a voice calling me.

"McDonough. Wait a minute." It was Joe Robbie, the owner of the Miami Dolphins. "I've been looking all over for you. I want to offer you a three-year no cut contract. We haven't had a block like that all year!"

Because I've spent most of my officiating time watching the quarterback and other backfield activity, I've seen quite a few spontaneous and effective lessons taught.

In the 1962 AFL All-Star game, George Blanda was quarterbacking the East team. On the first scrimmage play, a young guard came barreling through the line and knocked George down hard.

George reached up and grabbed the kid by the top of his jersey and explained patiently, "This is the All-Star game, sonny. Vacation starts tomorrow. Just bump me and I'll *fall* down."

Referees have to learn how to "play" a quarterback. By "play," I mean how far back (deep) you should line up to watch the action. You want to be close to it, but not part of it.

You're going to line up close to a pocket quarterback. He is one who either hands off or passes. You learn to give a scrambling quarterback more room, because he is capable of handing off to a running back, passing, or running with the ball himself, and frequently makes the decision as the play progresses. In my first game covering San Diego quarterback Jack Kemp, he taught me well. On a pass play, somehow I got caught between him and four big linemen and wound up on my butt. I was still able, though, to see him intentionally ground the ball. As I was stepping off the penalty he complained to me, "How could you see the pass when you were in there on the bottom of the pile?"

I said, "Don't give me any static, Jack, or I'll quit blocking for you." Later in the game, he ran the same play; however, this time it worked for a touchdown. As I threw up my arms to signify the score, he turned to me and said, "Nice blocking, Big Ref."

Jack later had a great career quarterbacking the Buffalo Bills. He no longer throws passes today, he catches them from all angles. He is a United States Congressman from New York.

My method of handling quarterbacks like Kemp, John Hadl, Fran Tarkenton and others who were prone to ducking out of the "pocket" was simply to position myself an extra five yards behind them. There was little chance that George Blanda or Joe Namath would run over you. Players like Len Dawson or Terry Bradshaw, however, who would run when trapped, taught you to be ready to get out of the traffic.

There was no way I wanted to get close to a backfield that had such swift and agile runners as a Paul Lowe, Mike Garrett, or Mercury Morris. These types of runners have fantastic balance. Just when it looked like I should blow the whistle to stop the play, they just might be getting an extra gift of balance and be off for another eight or ten yards.

The only way the guys in the striped shirts can lose is if they get too close.

TWO

When do centers get any recognition? I mean, who knows who the center on a football team is? Quarterbacks wouldn't even recognize them on the streets unless they were bending over.

I wasn't always a referee. I started out as a center. No one else wanted to be knocked down as soon as they put their heads through their legs, and because I was one of the biggest kids I played that position from the seventh grade all the way through junior college and at Stanford.

As far as I know, I still hold the record for the most minutes played in the Rose Bowl—not on New Year's Day—but regular season for Pasadena Junior College. Shav Glick, who is now one of the top sportswriters in the Los Angeles area, was then the sports editor of the Pasadena Junior College Chronicle. He sent that important bit of trivia in to Ripley's *Believe It Or Not.*

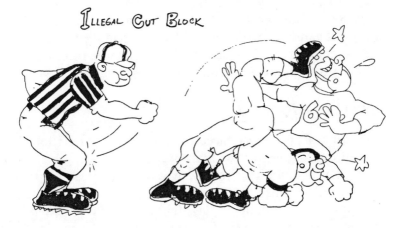

ILLEGAL CUT BLOCK

During World War II, Frank Leahy, the Notre Dame coach, and I were sitting in the officers' club on Ford Island in Pearl Harbor. Suddenly a young ensign sitting across from us turned to his shipmate and said, "Hey, look at this in *Believe It Or Not*. Here's a guy named John McDonough, who played 1080 minutes of football in the Rose Bowl." Frank Leahy laughed and said to the ensign, "Would you like to shake hands with John McDonough? This is John right here."

I scored a touchdown during that time, also. No, not as a center. It was on defense. One of my teammates, Bill Schulke, had intercepted a pass on the six yard line. He ran it

15

back to the ten, swung around and lateralled it to me. Ninety yards later it was a touchdown and time for me to turn my application in for halfback. In the hugging and the piling on that accompanies most unexpected touchdowns, someone yelled, "How in the hell did you do it?"

"I had to. Did you see the size of those guys chasing me? They looked like they were going to kill me."

My coach, Bob McNeish, took me out the last five seconds of my last game for PJC. When I left the field the public address announcer, Earl Ricker, made it even more memorable and beautiful for me by announcing my playing statistics.

LIFE ON THE FARM

The next season I experienced the reverse of that elation. I was third-string center for Stanford. I was playing behind Tony Calvelli and Louie Tsoutsouvas (All-American Unpronounceable). It wasn't until the end of the season, and then not until the last minute of play, that I was called to go into the game. As I ran onto the field for my debut, the public address announcer wound up with, "Ladies and gentlemen, soon you'll be driving home, and we want to caution you to please drive carefully." Although Tony and Lou were good friends, I was glad to see them graduate that year.

When do centers get any recognition? I mean, who knows who the center on a football team is. Quarterbacks wouldn't even recognize them on the streets unless they were bending over. And there I was trying to get myself out of football anonymity as a center and the announcer was talking about how the fans should be careful on their way home.

The pro scouts didn't make any special reports on me. There weren't any offers for me to play for pay. I was in and out of so few Stanford games, so quickly, that no one got a chance to see what I could do. I am not blaming anybody. I certainly deserved to play third string my first year on The Farm. The few minutes I played in 1937 didn't count against me so I got an extra year's eligibility. I played some in 1938 and in 1939 coach Tiny Thornhill switched me to tackle and I started three games.

It was tough in those days because of the substitution rule. If you came out of a game you couldn't return until the next quarter. Coaches had a tendency to stay as long as they could with their starters. If we had had the unlimited substitution rule that they have today, I'm confident I would have been one of the best offensive centers around because I was an excellent blocker and could snap the ball with deadly accuracy on punts and place kicks. I could also kick off right through the end zone, but kicking specialists were unheard of in the 1930s. It took a lot of humility to stay on the bench without going crazy, game after game.

I fully empathize with those players who couldn't take it and have run right into the game, uncalled upon by their coach. Even if you know the guys playing ahead of you at your position are better than you, even though you know that the game is all part of a total group effort and university cause; all "that you know" doesn't count. You're still sitting there, or as it is in most college and pro games now, standing there. It takes guts to keep telling yourself that you have to keep yourself ready to go into the game when you know you may never get called. Coaching staffs should be as concerned with the psyches of the non-playing suited-up-for-the-game players as they are with the playing-players, in getting them ready for a winning effort.

Of course, if Frankie Albert had missed any glory he thought was his, he would have stopped the game right there until he got it. The 1940 "Wow" boys of Coach Clark Shaughnessy had Frankie, Pete Kmetovic, Norm Standlee and Hugh Gallarneau. I was a senior when most of that great team and football dynasty at Stanford were only sophomores.

Frankie was one of the greatest quarterbacks in the country during those years. He was also famous for his pranks on coaches and officials. When he played for Stanford, the Los

Angeles Coliseum had its players' dressing room in a building outside the stadium. To get to the field you had to go through a tunnel and then down a steep flight of steps—fifty of them. Frankie could negotiate them well. On the way to a USC game he purposely fell down that flight of steps. Coach Clark Shaughnessy rushed through a crowd of players to get to him. Panic-stricken, he shook him, and horrified, hollered, "Frankie, Frankie! Are you all right?"

Very slowly Frankie opened his eyes and whispered, "I often wondered what you'd do if I got hurt."

Mark Duncan, who was Supervisor of Personnel for the NFL, tells the story of when Frankie was playing with the San Francisco 49ers. One of the assistant coaches on the 49ers was heckling the referee throughout the first half of the game. Finally the referee asked Frankie who the guy in the felt hat and tweed coat was. Frankie looked over at the man on the sidelines and said, "I never saw the guy before in my life."

The referee then went to the sidelines, summoned a police officer, and told him to escort the guy away from the bench area. The officer grabbed the assistant coach by the arm and began to take him out. When he resisted, and tried to explain who he was, another officer came over to help.

I always wished I had Frankie's nerve. I might have taken the non-glory right out of centering.

THE EARLY YEARS

Beth Lamb, my sweetheart since high school, and I were married the day after Frankie Albert and the Wow boys defeated Nebraska in the 1941 Rose Bowl. It was the year after I graduated from Stanford at the end of my first season as the head coach of McCloud High School. The school was at the base of Mount Shasta in the Siskiyou mountains of northern California. The applicants for the job were so closely qualified, the only thing that stood out in my record was the fact that I was once an Eagle Scout. That tipped the job in my favor.

I got to the town on a Saturday and became concerned when I didn't see any kids around big enough to play football. Sunday was the same. I went to both churches and saw no one who would make the starting line, or any one I would allow to carry the ball during a game. On Monday, when school began, there they were—big and ready. They had been working in the forests as lumberjack's helpers for the summer.

One thing that keeps a lumber camp happy is a good cook in the company restaurant and this town had one. He was the biggest man around. His son, Stan Smith, was without a doubt the biggest and roughest player we had. He seldom got the guy who had the ball, but he knocked everyone else down so one of the defensive ends could come around and make the tackles. Both he and the end made All-League. The Smith kid was All-Everything. His dad came to every game wearing a long dark coat with the left pocket filled with silver dollars. On a good play he would call out to his son, "Great play, Stan," and take one or two silver dollars out of the left pocket and ceremoniously drop them into the right one. When Stan screwed up, he would take one or two away from the "good playing" pocket. After each game, the players would rush over to the cook to see how well Stan had done. The dollars in the right hand pocket were for them to use for their postgame party at the malt shop. The team played well enough for all of the money. Our record was 8-1.

The next year I was working in Crockett, California, at John Swett High School. I got a raise in salary of $400 to make my annual wage $2,000. My record there was also 8-1, but I learned more during one of the victories that year at McCloud than I did in any game I coached or officiated since.

Pop Warner came with me to that game and also taught me the lesson. My father, God rest his soul, had played for the Gallaudet School for the Deaf in 1901, when they played against the Carlisle Indian School. Pop Warner was Carlisle's coach then. Had it been a few years later, dad would have been playing against Jim Thorpe.

This particular game was played during deer-hunting season. Pop was up in the area but wouldn't go hunting on the weekend, because that was the time, he said, that the people from San Francisco came up and shot each other instead of the deer. High school games in the forest country of northern California were played on Saturdays. We would leave early in the morning and drive to the game, play it, and turn around at night to drive back home. It was enough to take Sunday right out of you.

Although we won that game 6-0, Pop told me I almost gave the game away because I was harassing the officials for missing a clipping foul. He told me that as soon as I let my players know that I was blaming the officials for one thing my players started to blame them for everything.

"They ran out of time on your six yard line. If you would have started getting on the officials earlier, they would have won the game," Pop said.

After that I never let myself or any of my players think the game was to be played against the guys in the striped shirts instead of the players on the other team. Since then I've lost count of the number of games I've seen lost by coaches who got on the officials, thereby giving their players a chance to alibi. High school kids, in particular, will go along, copying the behavior of their coach to get them through the game.

THE WAR YEARS

After the Crockett season, the war broke out and within six months I had accepted a commission as an ensign with the Navy. I went to Annapolis for training and then was assigned as an athletic officer and officer-in-charge of the shore patrol at the Livermore, California, Naval Air Station. The aviation cadets called us "muscle benders." In July 1944, just a month before our daughter Deveda Merrilyn was born I was promoted to lieutenant.

Later I was transferred to Pearl Harbor, as staff athletic officer for Admiral Ross E. Lockwood. Two of my roommates were football's George "Potsy" Clark and Frank

Leahy. Potsy was a pro coach in the thirties who distinguished himself by winning the first ten games he coached in the pros, for the Detroit Lions. The legendary Leahy has one of the greatest college coaching records in football history. We became lifelong friends.

We also shared many football stories. My favorite, of course, had to do with officials.

Once, while Frank was making an impassioned plea to his Notre Dame players at halftime, the field judge came in and told one of his assistants to tell him that there were five minutes left during halftime intermission. The assistant didn't tell Frank until it was too late for him to get his team out on the field in time and the Irish were penalized for being late for the kickoff.

When Frank objected, the field judge stepped in and told him, "Coach, I personally told your assistant."

"But, you didn't tell me," Frank objected.

The penalty stuck. Three weeks later, the same field judge came into the dressing room and Frank was in the midst of another rousing discourse. This time the field judge interrupted him and handed him a card.

"Read this, coach." The card said, "I have been notified of the five minute halftime warning."

Frank said, "O. K." and started to give the card back. The field judge handed him a pencil and said, "Now sign it."

After a stint in Guam I returned to Pearl Harbor in August of 1945. I got there just in time to take over the Sub Base baseball team. We won the championship. On my team I had Bob Sheffing, Schoolboy Rowe, Charlie Gilbert, and, near the end of the season, a marine flyer by the name of Ted Williams. How could we help but win? They made a hell of a coach out of me.

Surprisingly enough, with all the football games I have seen, the greatest athlete I have ever been associated with was a baseball player—Schoolboy Rowe. He suffered from excruciating arthritis in his back. It hurt him so badly that he could hardly sleep. I tried to get him out of the Navy on an early release but every time his case was considered, he told the medical board that when he returned to the States he would go down to Hot Springs, Arkansas, take the baths there, and, "When my back gets better I'll report to Detroit to start playing baseball." The board couldn't let him go because they would be accused of giving baseball players priority over other servicemen.

Venom from bee stings was used to help arrest the arthritis. As painful as it was, he still played. He was a great athlete, but what I admired most about him was that he felt a tremendous responsibility to play his sport. I used to shake my head in disbelief every time I watched him pitch. A chill went through me every time he insisted on going out to the mound to perform.

HOME AGAIN

After the war I worked at the Pasadena Veterans Administration as a training officer. Our son, Joel, was born in 1947, and named after Joel "Tex" Middleton, who was a great inspiration to me throughout my life. He was the man who had recruited me for Stanford.

At that time in Pasadena I coached American Legion baseball and was proud to have on my team Bobby Lillis and Dick Williams, players who made it big in the pro ranks.

In September of 1947 I became Coordinator of Physical Education for the Orange County Department of Education. Little did I know then that I would sign twenty-six more contracts and that semirural Orange County would become the second largest population center in California. My responsibilities grew right along with it. In 1947 I knew the first name of every school principal in the county. By 1974 I couldn't name all the schools let alone their principals. In all those years I never gave up the responsibility for physical education. That was the fun part of the job and I always took care of it personally.

My last five years in the department I was the Assistant Superintendent in charge of the Operations Division. As such, I became the administrator for the six schools we operated inside the county's juvenile institutions in addition to my other duties. Our excellent staff of principals and teachers tried to strengthen the weak spots in each boy's and girl's education so they could compete on a par with their classmates in their home school when the judge released them.

I remember the principal of one of my mountain camp schools calling me one day to excitedly report that his boys had won their high school league championship in cross country running.

"You mean you're teaching those kids to run cross country?" I asked.

Quickly he replied, "Don't worry, John, we have several counselors and a couple of deputy sheriffs along the way to make sure they stay on the course and stop when they finish."

Also, I was the administrator of seven schools for the mentally retarded and handicapped children. The education of these special children is one of the hardest, most demanding, and taxing teaching jobs there is. The patience, skill, love and dedication of teachers and young teachers' aids often had me driving from their schools back to my office with a lump in my throat.

Besides these schools I still took care of the physical education, worried about a hundred and seventy-five teachers and fifty support personnel plus a personal staff of five professionals and six secretaries, and managed a multi-million dollar budget.

On twenty weekends a year I refereed pro football and in my spare time I operated my home office where I assigned officials for all the sports in the county's high schools.

Beth used to say, "Of every ten people I meet, one knows you are the Assistant Superintendent of the Department of Education, about five know you are the high school commissioner, but they all know you referee professional football."

Suffice it to say that one of the reasons I got into officiating was to be closer to the action. When I was through with the "playing" part of my football career, what else could I do to get in the game? I had enough of coaching. Watching the local high school or college teams wasn't enough. Television hadn't come into my living room yet with all of its angles and close-ups. The most excitement I could get would be with the third team on the field—the one that turned out to be the most important to me—the officials. That way I could be a winner no matter which of the other teams won.

BREAKING INTO THE JOB

I had worked as a basketball official in northern California before the war. After the war, living in southern California, I joined the Orange County Officials Association and worked high school games in the area. That was about thirty years ago, and I had an experience then, early in my whistling career, that gave me a good taste of exactly what I was getting myself into.

I had finished working a game and there was no officials' dressing room in the stadium so I had to wear my uniform on the way home. Just as I was passing another high school field where a game had just ended, one of my tires went flat. There I was, on the side of a street, trying to put on the spare. Some of the kids from the "losing" school saw me and really let me have it. Eggs—tomatoes—grapefruit—shaving cream—the official's average postgame diet. Maybe that's why we don't smile much. All of it was meant for the kids from the winning school, but I was easier game. Later, kids from the winning school came by and wanted to use my car as a shield for the next time the losers circled the block. When they left, they gave me a dozen eggs and some advice, "Protect yourself."

In 1949, Vern Landreth, who was then retiring as an official with the Pacific Coast Conference (now the PAC-10), urged me to apply to the league for a striped-shirt position. I did and was accepted for the 1950 season. Because of an overabundance of officials, it was as difficult then as it is now for officials to work many major college games. A big season for an official then was about five or six games. I felt very fortunate to get one varsity and four freshman games a year.

EXPERIENCE, THE BEST TEACHER

I worked small college games during that time, also. A couple of them had enough action in them for me to want to be home before the game was over. One of those games never officially ended.

It was played between Whittier and Occidental, and the game was as dull as a stock market report. The scoring was lopsided and done at will. There were about fifty people right behind the visitors' bench who were riding the coach and his players with derogatory and obscene remarks.

We got down to only fifteen seconds left in the game, the score was 49-7, and the team ahead had the ball. Just as the quarterback started to call his signals on the line, one of the defensive linemen straightened up, stepped through the line and punched him right in the jaw.

Both benches emptied and everyone started looking for someone else to hit. The fans got into it while the officials tried to hold back a few. One coach was sitting on an opposing player on the ground, punching him. One of his players tried to kick the sat-upon player, missed, and kicked his own coach in the head.

As I backed off the field one of my officials hid behind me. Apparently he didn't want to get kicked in the head too. It was a matter of survival for everyone. Then I thought of the band. Yes, the band. I ran over and told the surprised band leader to start the music and he said, shocked and surprised, "Now, you want music, now?"

"Yes, dammit. Play *The Star-Spangled Banner*."

As soon as the band started playing, the players stopped fighting. It was magic. It was like a dirge. They stopped and looked apologetic as they started to walk off the field, like little kids waiting for their parents to yell at them for what they had done. There may have been yelling later, but the final fifteen seconds of that game have still not been played.

Another game that year ended just as unbelievably. The only difference was that the fighting was verbal and that neither of the people fighting were players. The game was close and the opposition was about two points down, right at the end. It was in another small college game, between Occidental and a school I won't identify, because I don't want to embarrass them.

On the last play of the game, as soon as one of the players on the other team was tackled, he turned over and started to moan and groan and kick, holding his stomach. There were about four ticks left on the clock.

I leaned over him and said, "Take it easy, the trainer is coming." Before I could finish, the gun went off and the game was over.

Out comes this man yelling and screaming hysterically at me. He came right to me, ignoring the kid on the ground. He was shouting "That man was injured! Why didn't you stop the clock? You're supposed to stop the clock! When a man is injured you're supposed to stop the clock!"

I couldn't believe it, "How fast am I supposed to do it? The guy hit the ground, turned over and yelled, and the gun went off."

"Well, you're not God and you can't decide whether that guy is injured or not. I am a doctor, the team doctor, and that man is injured!" When he finally ran out of breath I said, "Wait a minute, you mean to tell me you're the team doctor?"

"That's right," he said.

"If you're the team doctor then you shouldn't be worrying whether or not I stopped the clock; you should be treating your patient. But I've got news for you. Just as you passed him, your patient jumped up and ran for the dressing room. And if you go in there to catch him right now you might get him before he gets on the bus."

His mouth fell open and he whirled around and left. Even the team doctor, who really is part of the official family, and responsible for keeping the game in good hands, can lose his cool. He convinced me I'd never want anybody but the referee in complete control of the game.

READING BETWEEN THE LINES

Referees have the license to do anything they can for the good of the game. The rule book doesn't mention remedies for everything that can possibly happen on the field, so we have to do whatever we feel is necessary, according to our common sense, wits and feel for decency, to keep the show going.

In a bowl game I worked, one player must have thought that since there wasn't a specific rule against rubbing mud into an opponent's face, he therefore had permission to do it.

He was wrong. I threw a flag. The coach screamed, "What the hell was that for?"

"Fifteen yards. Unsportsmanlike Conduct."

"For what?"

"For rubbing mud in his face." I pointed to the mud-faced player.

"Where does it say that in the book?"

"It doesn't. But if a kid wants to push his own face into the mud, that's his business. When he starts doing it to another player's face, that's my business. It's unsportsmanlike, and doesn't belong here."

"You show me where it says that."

I didn't answer him.

"I better find it when I look." he continued.

"You won't find Mud-in-the-Face in the rule book but you might find it in your play book."

THREE

"We are the players, but they are in control. It is as if they are saying to us, 'You are the performers, but we are in control.'"

Jon Staggers, II, former wide receiver, Green Bay Packers

BIG REF

Along with working in the Orange County school system all week and chasing a bunch of kids all over a football field on weekends, I was a disc jockey. It was on station KWIZ in Santa Ana, California. People would call in and ask me questions on sports and I would answer them and spin some records. I also gave out questions to the sports fans, and people who called in with the right answers would win a flashlight or a pair of tickets to a football game or whatever. Well, one day, after I had been doing this for about a year, a fan called in and asked for "the Big Ref." After we finished talking, the station manager, Hal Davis, decided Big Ref would be the name of the show.

DELAY OF GAME

"You're going to be known as the Big Ref," he said. It's a name that has hung with me since then. It was Hal Davis who told me one day he had read in the paper that there was going to be a meeting at the Beverly Hilton Hotel with some people who were going to organize a new pro football league called the American Football League. He asked me if I had enough time to stop by and get a story. I agreed, but I had no idea how much "time" I was getting myself into.

THE AMERICAN FOOTBALL LEAGUE

I went to the meetings and during their press conferences I met Bud Adams, owner of the Houston Oilers; Lamar Hunt, the owner of the Kansas City Chiefs (which was then the Dallas Texans); and Barron Hilton, owner of the San Diego Chargers (which was then the Los Angeles Chargers). I was very impressed at their determination. A few weeks later I picked up the paper and read that Joe Foss, the great marine ace, and the former Governor of South Dakota, was the first commissioner of the American Football League. The paper also stated that Bob Austin, former National League referee, would be the Supervisor of Officials. Their league office headquarters would be in Dallas. Well, what did I have to lose?

I wrote a letter telling them I was interested in being an official. They sent me an application which I filled out and returned but didn't hear from them again for quite awhile. In the meantime I found out that a good friend of mine, Jim Tunney, had also applied to both the NFL and AFL. Nothing happened for a while until I got another letter asking for additional information.

Again, a period of waiting, then a telephone call from Bob Austin, in Chicago. He set up a time for me to meet with him at the Los Angeles airport.

I didn't get a physical description of him but when I saw a big ruddy-faced guy get off the plane I figured it must be him. I was right. He interviewed me and said he would get in touch with me. I thought that might be as far as I was going to get with the league, but I still had some hope. Soon I heard from Jim that he had been hired by the National Football League. In fact, Jim is still working with the league and is the only referee who worked two successive Super Bowl games, 1977 and 1978. A day after I talked to Jim I got a call from Bob Austin asking if I was still interested in being an official. I said, "Yes."

"Your contract is in the mail," he said.

Well, the contract came and it was for two thousand dollars for the first season. That was a lot more than I had ever received working in the college ranks. Bob told me later that because I was the first official in the league to sign and return a contract he gave me the lowest number, #11, which I kept until I retired.

My friends told me I was crazy. The National League would bury these people in the new league. "No way it's going to make it."

I told them that I was betting it would be different.

They had good reason to think that way. There had been other leagues in the history of pro football to challenge the existing National Football League that did not last. Three of them were called the American Football League, coincidentally (1920, 1936, 1940). One of them was called the All-American Football Conference (1946). The teams in those leagues either became part of the National League or disbanded due to lack of serious fan support.

Things started to jell for the AFL this time. We had our first officials' clinic, in Dallas, Texas, and I was appointed as a referee of a five man crew. On our crew was Clyde Devine, the umpire, who was my supervising teacher when I was a student teacher at Sequoia High School in Redwood City, California. Clyde had worked in the old All-American Conference and then in the National Football League and here he was with us in the beginning of the American Football League. Elvin Hutchison was the head linesman. He, too, had been in the National Football League. He and Gil Castree had told Bob Austin they would come over to the new league and help him break in the new pro officials. We were very fortunate to have Elvin and his experience on our crew. We nicknamed him "Pappy."

Our line judge was Willard "Lefty" Goodhue, one of the top officials in southern California. Our field judge was Chuck Liley, a highly regarded college official from Denver, Colorado. There were only five men on a crew then. In 1962 the AFL followed the lead of the NFL and added a sixth man, the back judge, and in 1978, the seventh man, the side judge was added.

The AFL games were more wide-open than the NFL. Scores were higher. There were only three man front lines on defense, and zone defenses were used. The moving pocket was an innovation of the AFL. For the fans, there was the added luxury of knowing who each player on the field was by having his name stamped right on the back of his jersey. Fifty years earlier Pop Warner had the idea of putting numbers on jerseys. The AFL was also the first pro league to make the electric scoreboard clock the official time.

The first game we ever worked in the American Football League was on the night of July 31, 1960, in Kezar Stadium, San Francisco, between the Dallas Texans (now the Kansas City Chiefs) and the Oakland Raiders. Dallas won 20-13. I remember when I first walked into the sparsely filled stadium, I thought, "I hope they didn't print too many programs." It was cold, miserable and foggy. The game films showed us disappearing into and reappearing out of the fog. If the word about the league wasn't strong enough to get people to come out and see us, then the fog was the best place for us to play.

We played an exhibition game in Sacramento, California, between the Oakland Raiders and the Titans (now the New York Jets) and we couldn't even give away our complimentary tickets. Each official was given two tickets to give to friends, relatives, or people we met along the way. This practice is also done in the National Football League. In the beginning of the American League, sometimes we would give the tickets back to the front office or the man at the ticket gate, because we couldn't find anyone to give them to.

Things have changed. Sometimes it seems like you just can't win. I remember once I was walking into the Coliseum in Los Angeles to work a college game and some guy from my hometown yelled through the fence to ask me if I had a couple of extra tickets. I told him, "No, in fact, I had to buy a couple extra for my two kids." That was true. Later I discovered that he told everybody he had seen me over at the Coliseum and I had plenty of tickets but wouldn't give him any. I learned a long time ago if I hear someone calling my name when I'm walking into a stadium to keep walking and not pay any attention. Once I am inside, if I hear someone call me, I'll look to see who it is and wave or say hello if there is time. Friends who are inside the stadium already have tickets!

In the first year of the AFL there were a number of players who were free agents, having played out their string in the NFL. Some of the AFL clubs signed them as players but they knew that part of their job was to help teach the rookies about pro football. They were referred to as "retreads."

A number of these retreads got the idea that they were going to punch and kick their way through this new, upstart league. The officials had another idea. During that first year I kicked fifteen players out of games, for playing something other than football. In the next thirteen years that I officiated pro ball, I didn't kick out more than five players, total.

One particular player, that first year, I kicked out of two games. He didn't last through the first quarter in each contest. Prior to the third game he came over to me and asked if I "had it in for him."

I said, "No. As a matter of fact, I'd like to see you play a whole game, but you can't keep slugging and kicking people and stay in this league." He didn't kick or slug anybody that day and after the game he came up to me and asked, "How did I do?"

"You did just great. I am proud of you. And so are the guys you didn't beat the hell out of."

In the beginning of the AFL there were only eight teams. The officiating crews were made up of men who came from the same general area. My crew was made up of men from California with the exception of Chuck Liley from Denver. The second year, 1961, Ben Dreith, also from Denver, was switched to our crew to replace Liley. We were known as the Hollywood crew. We worked games that were in the western part of the country. Most of them were in Oakland, San Diego or Denver. We went a long time without going east of Dallas, Houston or Kansas City. When we started going further east it was usually on a double swing, like a Saturday game in Miami and a Sunday game in Buffalo. With the present schedule in the NFL, an official might work in the same city only once in two or three years. That's a great way to have it.

In 1964 we worked three consecutive home exhibition games in Oakland, had two of their games on the road, skipped a week, and returned to their home field the following week to open their regular season play against the Kansas City Chiefs. My crew worked so often in Oakland I was afraid they would award me a "Block O" at the end of the season.

On September 27, the day of the Kansas City game, I was standing in the end zone waiting for the television people to let me know when to start the kickoff. I happened to glance over to the Chiefs' coach, Hank Stram. He was pointing at me and holding his nose. I wondered what that was all about until Frank Kirkland, our field judge, pointed behind me. I looked and there was a bunch of fans holding a long piece of butcher paper that said

'WELCOME HOME, BIG JOHN,
WE LOST LAST WEEK.'

As officials from the west coast, one of the things we had to deal with was being accused of favoring western teams in eastern stadiums. Another concern then was that the entire crew rode on the same airplane. What if the plane got diverted, ran into bad weather, or heaven help us, crashed? When the leagues merged, the NFL changed things so that a crew was not made up of officials who came from the same area. This reduced the potential travel problems. If a plane with an official aboard is grounded by a snowstorm there will be enough officials to run the game. I've heard the comment that if the officials don't show the people would be understanding, but I don't buy that. If one of the teams doesn't show the people will be understanding. You can't play the game without the other team, but if the officials don't show the people will want to know why the league doesn't have an extra set of men waiting to get on the field. The idea of having two crews of officials on hand would be economically unfeasible. Figure it out. Twenty-eight teams, fourteen games, and seven officials each game. One of the biggest expenses of the NFL is the employment and transportation of officials. Double that cost to have an extra set of officials at each game? Go ahead!

What would happen if there was a game and none of the officials showed?

FOUR

*"Watch the sidelines,
Make sure they keep their hands in
and don't listen to the criers."*

On August 4, 1972, in a preseason game between the Rams and Browns, the Browns received the kickoff and on their first play from scrimmage they threw an interception. One of the Rams ran it in for a touchdown. The Rams kicked off again and the Browns ran one series of downs and punted. We gave a time-out to the television crew and the Cleveland defensive unit came in for its first play. A rookie for the Browns came up to umpire Walt Parker, and said, "Hey, Ref, watch number 68. He's been holding the whole game."

Walt looked straight at the rookie and said, "What did you say?"

The rookie repeated his statement, "Watch number 68, 'cause he's been holding the whole game."

36

Holding

I said, "For your information, neither you nor number 68 has played one down in this game, yet."

The rookie looked at us chagrined, and admitted sheepishly, "That wasn't too sharp, was it?"

Walt replied, "No, and if you're going to try and con us you ought to play a couple of downs first."

Now, when I called Walt Parker an umpire, you probably thought, "Umpire? I thought they only had them in baseball. They call them referees in football." Well, TV and radio people and even players and coaches call all of us refs, but actually there are seven zebras on the field, the third team—the crew—the officials in the striped shirts.

Besides the referee and umpire, there are five other officials in pro football. The linesman, the line judge, the back judge, the side judge and the field judge. Here is a very brief rundown on their primary duties.

First some general things about the crew:

1. Prior to each game they decide how they will adjust in the event that one of them is injured during the game.

2. They wear the uniform prescribed by the league office.

3. The entire crew arrives at the stadium dressing room one and a half hours prior to the kickoff. Once the crew has arrived no one is allowed in their dressing room except persons specifically authorized by the commissioner. The restriction includes owners and coaches.

4. All officials have equal jurisdiction over fouls. They do not have an area of the field as their sole coverage.

5. The entire crew is responsible if there is an error in the mechanics or the interpretation of a rule.

6. The crew arrives on the playing field ten minutes prior to kickoff.

7. The officials are the representatives of the commissioner and have complete jurisdiction over the game. All players, coaches, sideline personnel, stadium personnel and the police are expected to cooperate with them.

Now let's take a look at each specific position:

THE REFEREE

1. The referee is the crew chief and is the final authority on all matters not specifically assigned to other officials by the Rule Book or the Mechanics Manual. At the start of each play, he positions himself behind and to the right of a right-handed quarterback and to the left of a left-handed quarterback.

2. The referee conducts the coin toss three minutes prior to the kickoff. He signals which team will receive prior to

the start of the game and at the beginning of the second half.

3. The referee explains all fouls and their options to the captains, indicates all choices by the proper signal, and administers all penalties. If the enforcement is obvious he may administer the penalty without explanation to the captains.

4. He personally notifies the coach when one of his players has been disqualified and designates one of the other officials to notify the opposing coach.

5. He notifies the captain and the head coach when they have used up their allowable time-outs and at the two minute warning.

6. The referee will raise his arm, chop it down, and sound his whistle to start every thirty second count. This is often referred to as declaring the ball "ready for play."

THE LINESMAN

1. The linesman sets up his chain and downbox crew on the side of the field selected by the referee. He works that side of the field the first half and the opposite side the second half.

2. The box and chain crew are under the direct supervision of the linesman. They operate, without deviation, according to the instructions he has given them.

3. He is primarily responsible for encroachment and offsides and other action in and around the line. He is also responsible for the forward progress of the ball, for his sideline down to the side judge, and he aids the umpire in checking for ineligible linemen going downfield.

4. He counts the players on the offense on every play.

THE LINE JUDGE

1. The line judge works on the line of scrimmage on the opposite side of the field from the linesman.

2. He has overall responsibility for the supervision of the timing of the game and the electric clock operator is directly responsible to him. In the event the electric clock malfunctions he takes over the timing on the field.

3. He is responsible for knowing if the passer throws from behind the line and for checking illegal motion behind the line. He rules on all illegal shifts.

4. He fires his pistol at the end of each quarter.

5. He performs the same duties as the linesman in item three of his instructions, except the portion of the sideline covered by the back judge.

6. He times the halftime intermission and notifies the home team coach when there are five minutes remaining.

THE BACK JUDGE

1. The back judge works approximately seventeen yards downfield on the line judge's side of the field.

2. He is responsible for the sideline downfield on his side.

3. He counts the number of players on the defensive team on each play.

4. On pass plays he covers the area on his side behind the umpire.

5. On field goals and conversions he covers the goal post on his side and judges if the kick is between the uprights and over the crossbar.

6. He keeps a written record of all time-outs, why they occurred and whether or not television used the time for a commercial.

THE FIELD JUDGE

1. The field judge works approximately twenty-five yards downfield near the midline.

2. He is primarily responsible for the ball, the legality of the tee, and the kicker on all free kicks.

3. He is responsible for all kicks, passes, and runs that come into his area.
4. He times the thirty second count and the two minute intermission at the end of the first and third quarters.
5. He notifies the visiting coach five minutes prior to the end of the halftime intermission.
6. On field goals he teams with the back judge on ruling the field goal successful or unsuccessful.

THE SIDE JUDGE

Note: At the beginning of the 1978 season, the NFL added a seventh official, the side judge.

1. The side judge is about seventeen yards downfield on the same side as the linesman.
2. He is responsible for the sideline downfield on his side.
3. On pass plays he will cover the area on his side behind the umpire.
4. He will be assigned other duties as time goes on.

THE UMPIRE

1. The umpire is usually four to six yards beyond the scrimmage line in the defensive backfield.
2. His primary duty is to supervise the play of the offensive and defensive interior linesmen.
3. Prior to the game he will inspect all bandages, braces, and pads and pass on their legality according to rule. The umpire is the final judge on all matters pertaining to equipment.
4. He assists the referee on all close line play and in setting up the ball and keeping it dry, for the next play.
5. He must know and rule on all ineligible linemen downfield on a pass.
6. After a running play or a pass play goes by, the umpire will turn and "clean up" behind it.

We call him the diplomat of the crew because he is the only guy who starts each play with people behind him. And by people, I mean football players. And, if you're going to work in front of a Dick Butkus all afternoon or night, you're going to be a diplomat, I'll guarantee you. The umpire is responsible for everything that goes on up in the front lines, the holding, shoving and all the illegal grabbing. I was an umpire once for two games and was more than happy to return to my position as referee. Glad to work back there watching the offensive backfield, making sure the guys coming to get the quarterback did it "honestly," and letting everyone know when he was throwing the ball deliberately to the ground.

The major universities use a six man team of officials. In the small colleges there are five. One acts as a back judge and field judge. In high school there are only four officials. There are no downfield officials, which means the two officials on each sideline have to be ready to run like hell after some kid who's probably a sixteen-year-old sprint champion.

To keep in emotional balance and psychological shape during a game, officials need to look for humor, wherever they can find it.

Officials are considered part of the game, and that means that they should be treated by players during a play as if they weren't even there. If an official is tackled along with other players, it's unfortunate, an unpleasant ride to the ground, but there is no penalty. If one of us gets tackled out in the open field, deliberately, then it might be the last tackle that player gets paid to make. He'll probably get kicked out of the league.

I was working a game with Clyde Devine as the umpire. The Denver quarterback, Fred Tripucka, threw a pass that landed right in Clyde's stomach. Clyde caught it and quickly threw it on the ground. Tripucka turned to me and yelled, "Tell your umpire to get out of the way!"

"Well, don't throw the ball into his stomach or he'll catch it every time."

On the next play he connected with his own end for a touchdown and spent the rest of the afternoon trying to convince me that the Clyde pass was purely unintentional.

Barry Brown was the umpire on our crew for two years. He had a strong officiating personality. He would "sell" his calls well. He had momentum, force and strength when he made a tough call. We worked together very successfully and had many occasions for hard-hitting laughter.

In one game Barry got knocked down, damn near killed, from a mixture of quick linebackers and blockers. I ran by to see if he was all right, and when I saw he was beginning to recuperate, I asked him, "How do things look from down there?"

He told me what I could do with myself, and five minutes later, when I was flat on my back from a block I got while watching somebody plant the quarterback into the grass, he asked me the same question.

I told him what he could do with himself, but he said it was anatomically impossible. A player who heard our exchange said, "What's the matter, here. Don't you guys like each other?" Officials don't have to smile out there, but we did.

Another umpire I had with me one year though, didn't think it was a bit funny when our head linesman kept coming out after each play and repositioning the ball. The umpire or the referee are the only ones who are supposed to spot the ball. This head linesman was a bit too officious for an official. It got so bad that I had to restrain the umpire from going after him. Can you imagine that very human possibility? The officials going at each other and the players stepping in between to break them up.

No one is allowed in the officials' dressing room, before the game, at half time, or after the game. There have been exceptions, but the league office wants to know about them. It used to be required that if a coach or an assistant coach came into the room, we would note the time, what they wanted, and how long they stayed, and include this with our game report.

The people from television, or the public address announcer, may have to come by to get some information, like the names of the officials working the game. Other than that no one should be there, except the officials. I don't think it was more than four or five times in all the time that I worked in pro football that a coach came by to see the officials in their dressing rooms.

Once, Eddie Erdelatz, the first coach of the Raiders, came in and wanted to know what he should do because his team forgot to bring their long stockings. The rules require that they be worn by the players. I told him that we certainly weren't going to cancel the game because his equipment manager had forgotten to bring them. I also assured him that the other coach would know, and so would the league office. The news would be in my game report.

Officials don't frequent a team's locker room either; however, sometimes it's unavoidable.

Randy Vataha, who played his high school and junior college football a few miles from my home, went on to Stanford and made All-Pac-8 and All-Coast as a wide receiver. The Rams drafted him in 1971 and cut him after the third preseason game. He was only 5'10'' and 170 pounds soaking wet. Nine days prior to the first league game, the New England Patriots signed him.

I went back to Foxboro on Sept. 26, 1971, to work the second game ever played in their new stadium between the Patriots and the Detroit Lions. They were still working on the hallway to the officials' dressing room so we had to go through the Pats' quarters to get to ours.

As I walked into the Patriot dressing room there was little Randy Vataha sitting in his shorts and T-shirt right next to defensive tackle Houston Antwine, a six-footer who weighed 270 pounds. It looked like Antwine had brought the little kid next door to the game.

I walked up to Vataha and said, "Hey, Randy, the punt, pass, and kick kids are dressing on the other end of the stadium."

He said, "Oh, okay, John" and he leaned over, picked up his gear and started for the door.

That year as a rookie, he played in all fourteen games, caught 51 passes for 872 yards, and 9 touchdowns. And he probably had trouble convincing the security guards he belonged in the dressing room.

The Los Angeles Coliseum dressing room for officials still has the combination of my padlock on one of its walls. I wrote it there over twenty years ago. Since I kept all of the valuables of the crew I was working with in my locker, my staff would know how to get into my locker if for some reason I got carried out of the game. With the advent of more stadiums I put the combination on the inside of my belt, so that if they carried me out, one of the crew could look to see what the numbers were. I had told my wife that if she saw the crew start to take off my belt, I was hurt badly.

The last regular season game that I worked was between the New York Giants and the Minnesota Vikings. It was played in Harvard Stadium, which is probably one of the most archaic parks of the modern era. The game was played there because Yankee Stadium was being repaired, and the new home of the Giants in New Jersey was not officially available.

When we got there we found that we had to dress in an athletic building that was quite a distance from the playing field. As we walked across the long field to get to the stadium, we got a lot of advice from the New York fans on how we ought to call the game.

It was a day of bitter cold, one of those days when it snows and then rains and then snows and rains again. I remember the Viking team coming out onto the field, looking absolutely awesome in their big purple uniforms. On a freezing, snowy, gray day, those uniforms make the players look twice as big as they are. They were followed by their assistant coaches who were wrapped in their leather jackets with huge fur collars up around their necks. Then came Coach Bud Grant in a short sleeve shirt. There were no lights at the stadium and when I talked to both coaches about the possibility of having to shorten the game because of darkness, Coach Grant said there was nothing to worry about, that it wasn't all that bleak. We finished the game but every moment of the second half I thought darkness would descend and leave us looking for the football and the way out.

The officials were given a small room to stay in before the game and at half time. It was the groundskeeper's room, filled with lime and old cans of paint. It was a closet, really, and there shouldn't have been more than five people in it, but a lot more packed into it when we came in at halftime. There was no other place to stay warm.

Sparse? Yes. Not even enough quiet for the officials to have their halftime meetings. People crowded in right with us and it was so cold I didn't have the heart to tell them to leave. We asked one of the attendants at the stadium where the men's room was and he told us that we would have to go outside the stadium and on up to another building. One of the crew got up to leave and I grabbed his arm and said, "You can't go out there through all that crowd with your uniform on."

Before he could say anything, someone in the primitive ethic suggested to him that he use one of the empty paint cans. A voice from the other side of the room called out, "Hey, wait 'til I leave. I didn't know this was the men's room.

No one knew how she got there. The room was supposed to be for officials, but it turned out to be a place for anyone to get warm. And, no, I am not against women officiating in pro football. Women are already working high school games. I wouldn't be surprised to find out that they are working college games, too. I don't think it would do the pro game any harm to have women calling the foul shots and keeping order. In fact, their presence alone out there would probably cut the number of fouls and clean up the language.

Neither the officials nor the fans could laugh when the Patriots opened the 1971 season in brand-new Schaefer Stadium in Foxboro, Massachusetts. The stadium's plumbing wasn't working well, and what the system couldn't hold went overflowing into the aisles, down the steps and towards the field. Many suggested that the stench was our best critic, and at times I've been inclined to agree. The system was "probably" set up to get even. In the officials' dressing room, the urinals were installed where the sink was supposed to be, and vice versa. We had to think tall.

In a game in Denver, there was a mini rodeo exhibition at halftime. One of the horses left his opinion on the ground, and one of the players who noticed it on the first play of the second half wasn't impressed. He came over to me and wanted an immediate answer, "Do we have to play in that?"

"No," I said. "I'll get somebody to clean it up." Officials don't have to smile, but we're allowed to be cordial.

Umpires before a game will go up to both coaches, say hello, offer to shake hands, and ask each one if any of his players are wearing any unusual casts or bandages. They have to be checked, because we don't want anyone going out there and using any kind of external covering as a weapon.

Our umpire, Barry Brown, was asking Coach Tom Landry, of the Dallas Cowboys, if any of his players were wearing any protective equipment that needed to be checked for legality. The punter for Dallas was practicing his kicking along the sidelines and one of his practice shots landed right between Barry's eyes. Barry dropped to his knees and blood came pouring out of his nose. As he started to get up, Coach Landry said, "Just watch. The first foul called in the game will be against us and you'll probably be the one to call it."

It didn't take long for him to be right. On the third play of the game, Barry saw one of Tom's players commit a holding foul and Barry threw his flag immediately. And, no, the flag didn't fly to remind the coach of Barry's nose.

Prior to a college game years ago I went up to Coach Ben Schwartzwalder of Syracuse and asked him if he was going to do anything out of the ordinary, or different, that my staff ought to know about. He said he didn't plan to but when I started to walk away he said, "Wait a minute. If you get in the way of one of my players, be a blocker instead of a tackler. Last week one of the officials got in the way and knocked one of our ball carriers down. If it hadn't been for him we would have scored a touchdown."

I said, "I don't like to block or tackle anymore. I try to stay out of the way."

He said, "O. K., but if you're in the way, be a blocker, don't be a tackler."

I once asked Coach Paul Brown if there was anything unusual his team would do that premature judgment on our part might spoil.

He said, "No, nothing. Just straight football. We hope we're good enough to win."

And then on the very first play from scrimmage he ran a triple reverse for a touchdown. It had me jumping around like a disco dancer. After the conversion I came by Coach Brown on the sidelines and asked him, "You didn't think that was an unusual play?"

He smiled and said, "I forgot to tell you about that one."

Most officials will not talk to a coach who isn't courteous and respectful when he asks questions, protests or hyperactively complains. The best-selling dictionary might be compiled of all the obscene terms that have been contrived on the sidelines and thrown at officials in the quest for unlimited abuse.

A coach might be screaming at one official during an entire game and the official won't hear a word. He can tune him completely out. He has to. A coach might yell and worry himself into such a nervous trance or stupor that the next day, or even after the game, he won't be able to tell you one thing that he said to anybody during the game.

There are just a few times when the rules require officials to talk to coaches:

1. At the two minute warning—to find out who their captains are and tell them how many time-outs they have remaining.

2. Notification of a disqualified player.

3. To shorten the game or remaining periods due to darkness or some other extreme emergency.

4. Notification to the coach that his allowable three time-outs in the half have been taken.

Other than these instances, the designated captains are the sole representatives for their team in communications with officials.

Officials will talk to coaches to keep order or game control, and also to clarify some point about the rules. But it is a courtesy. It's none of this talk-to-the-talker, on demand.

If officials started listening to advice from coaches and players while the game is going on we'd all be trouble. I never minded listening to suggestions after a game about changing a particular ruling. In fact, I have been in favor of some of the ideas coaches have come up with. However, when I get into a game I am almost completely oblivious to the nervous complaining that comes from coaches and players in the bench area.

There aren't too many of them who know the rules and their nuances like the officials do. Coaches know strategies—manipulations of players. Who to keep, who to play here, and who not to play there. When to do this, and when not to. But they don't have the same perspective of the rules and the game we have. The assumptions players make about what is right and what should be right in the rules are often filled with misconceptions.

One coach made a cordial, quiet and sincere attempt to learn on the job and his attempt was dealt with full official hospitality. On January 29, 1966, George Wilson was hired as the first coach of the Miami Dolphins in the American Football League. He had compiled a record of 57-45-6 as head coach of the NFL Detroit Lions over an eight year span.

George did a fine job of starting his new team with a firm foundation, a team that later became one of the great teams in NFL history. He must have worked twenty hours a day for five and a half months to get ready to coach Miami's first game ever on August 6, 1966. It was a preseason game in San Diego, which the Dolphins lost 38-10.

I was the referee of that first game and midway through the second quarter Coach Wilson showed me a lot of class just after a Charger defensive back intercepted a Dolphin pass and took it into the end zone for a touchdown. About halfway through his run the defender dropped the ball, it hit on its flat side, bounced up and the man caught it and went in for the score.

After the conversion, Aaron Wade, our line judge, told me Coach Wilson wanted to talk to me.

I went over to him and he said, "I'm new in the AFL. Do your rules allow a player to pick up a fumble and run with it, like the NFL?"

I answered "Yes, coach, just like the NFL."

He replied, "Thank you, I was just checking."

He was a new coach in the AFL and that fine point in the rules hadn't come up so he was smart enough to find out right then in a gentlemanly way. He was my kind of coach.

On October 22, 1967, I went down to Miami to work a game between Miami and the New York Jets which the Jets won 33-14.

The game was "a can of corn" as we say in the officiating business. It's when there are no tough calls, the teams play well, it's an exciting contest, and everyone has a good time.

The thing I remember, with a grin, about the game was another incident with Coach Wilson. While we were waiting for the bands to get in place for the National Anthem I was standing on the Miami sidelines and I reached into my pocket and took out a roll of mints. A voice behind me asked, "What's that, John?" It was Coach Wilson.

"Mints, would you like one?"

"Sure."

"Here take two."

"Thanks."

"That's okay coach, we're always glad to be of service."

Well, the band played, we all sang, and I started the game.

Late in the second quarter I was standing in the middle of the field during a TV time-out and I took the roll of mints out of my pocket again and was just putting one in my mouth when I noticed George Wilson looking at me. I held up the mints as if offering him one and he smiled and nodded, "yes."

So, I trotted over to the sidelines and gave him a couple of more mints. A few minutes later I had to make a call that probably gave him more than mints could have soothed.

I have spoken to a number of officials' groups and clinics all over the country and the most important point I want to get across to them, especially the young guys, is that they are the *only* ones out there on the field who are getting *paid* to keep their "cool."

"One of the things you should never do is lose your composure, no matter how bad things get. You are the guys who have to keep everything under control."

I've never heard of an owner of a ball club fining his coach for yelling at his players because he got all excited. I've never heard of a coach fining or suspending any one of his players because they got all excited and started screaming at people. He wants them excited because it's a very emotional type of game and he wants them up for it. But an official? Absolutely not. The wilder and hairier it gets the more composed he has to be. If a guy wants to be a top official he has to know how to keep his "head" when everything around him is falling apart.

I have been known to get mad in a game but it was strictly for effect. I felt at that particular time that I needed to do it to get game control. There have been times when it was tough to keep from laughing at the shocked look in the players' and coaches' eyes.

During the preseason there's a lot of everything. A lot of fouls are called because players are "overplaying" in an effort to make the team. A lot of fans are upset because they've been forced to buy tickets to all of the preseason games if they want the option to buy their regular season tickets. A lot of players are on the sidelines, sometimes maybe twice as many as there are for the regular season games. And a lot of letters are sent by front-row fans to the league office telling them to keep the sidelines clear so that the close-sitting fans can see the game. We usually got a memo telling us to try to keep the crowded sidelines clean.

I was on a plane going to the Dallas at Philadelphia game in 1970 when I thought of a solution to the sideline problem. Barry Brown asked me about it and I told him I would let him know during the game when I would use it.

The answer came early in the first period. The linesman usually takes care of sideline problems. David Hawk, our linesman, had told the players to get back, away from the field. They did, but on the next play they jumped back to see what was happening on the field. A Dallas player had just turned the corner and was tackled and knocked back a few yards. The whole Dallas team was up and pointing to the place where they thought the ball should be spotted—which was where the linesman was going to place it anyway. Officials aren't out there asking for anybody's help. Somehow the crowd got the idea the Dallas team had conned him into placing the ball where it didn't belong, and they started to boo.

I looked over to Barry and said, "Here it comes."

I went over to the Dallas sideline and even surprised myself with how much energy and emphasis I put into it.

"All right, everybody, get back. Get back and sit down! You have to keep this area clear. Coach Landry and I have a job to do and we've got to keep it clear so I can see him and he can see me. So, get back and stay there!"

The coach turned around and told them all to get back, sit down and stay there. They did, and never got back up again. I turned to Barry and we both smiled.

"You conned them. You really conned them," he said.

"I didn't con anybody," I said, "but I gotta think of something new next time."

There was a time in pro football when a team was charged a time-out if the trainers came on for an injured player. This was to keep teams from taking advantage of calling a player injured when in effect they just wanted more time for player-coach conferences. If a trainer or doctor came onto the field it was considered an official team time-out and after three in one half, a team would be penalized five yards for every additional time-out—whether it was for an injury or not.

To keep their team from being charged with a time-out each time a trainer or doctor came onto the field, players began to haul injured players off the field. The mishandling of injured players brought on several lawsuits, so the rule was changed so that an injured player could have immediate medical attention.

Now, if an official sees an injured player he will stop the clock and beckon a trainer or doctor. These two people are the only ones who can touch, administer aid, or direct anyone to do anything to the injured player. The injured player must leave the game and the clock will not start until that player's replacement takes the field. I feel this is better for the game because it protects all players.

In one game, Coach Erdelatz, kept coming on the field every time there was an injured player. I cured him of that in a hurry when I stopped the clock after his third visit, and charged Oakland with a time-out. When I did, the Oakland captain, center Jim Otto, asked why I charged them a time-out.

"Your trainer is out on the field," I told him.

"That's not the trainer. That's the head coach," Otto said.

"When he comes out on the field to help an injured player he's the trainer." Otto ran to the coach and said, "Hey, coach, stay off the field, you're using up our time-outs." From that time on, Coach Erdelatz stayed off the field.

I once was guilty of causing a minor misunderstanding between a quarterback and his coach. I played in a golf tournament in Palm Springs with Roman Gabriel. We were in the partners' best-ball contest for the daily prize of a couple of television sets. When we came to the last hole, all Gabe had to do was sink a three-foot putt for us to win. Gabe ringed two putts before he got the ball in the cup and we didn't win anything. That was in May. In October, the Rams were playing the Falcons in Los Angeles, and Gabriel was quarterbacking.

He went to throw on one play and when he couldn't find a receiver, he dumped the ball off where nobody was. I threw a flag for intentionally grounding the ball.

"That's got to be the crappiest call in America," Gabe yelled at me.

"Yeah, just like the dumb putts you missed in Palm Springs." We both started to laugh.

Ram coach George Allen hollered, "What's going on out there with you guys?"

Gabe replied, "Nothing, coach. We're talking about golf."

Coach Allen showed me a lot of class when he shook his head and walked away.

I get a kick out of people who say an official has a short fuse, or blames them for getting "thin under the skin" whenever someone on the bench gets stuck with a fifteen yard penalty for various verbal abuses. The coach who gets an "unsportsmanlike conduct" call has probably had several warnings. In some cases, the coach may want the foul.

It was late in the game and this coach's team was getting trounced. (I am not going to mention his name because he still may be coaching.) I was working hard between plays talking to his players, reminding them they were pros and to play with some pride and not lose their poise. Sometimes you have to do this to keep the game from getting sloppy and possibly winding up in a fight.

I had the feeling that the coach was out to get me to give him a bench penalty of fifteen yards so he could look like a martyr on TV to the people back home. The closest I got to him all afternoon, besides hearing his constant screaming and complaining, was when I called a foul on one of his players that was right near the bench.

The ribbing got worse. Louder and more accusative, until I finally looked up at him and said, "Coach, I know you want fifteen. It will make you look like a martyr back in your own hometown, but I am not going to make you a martyr. Maybe the commissioner will take care of you on Monday." The reverse psychology worked. He calmed down for the rest of the game. I almost smiled.

FIVE

*Everyone stands for the kick-off
to sing the National Anthem—the
theme for the adrenalin of
anticipation.*

I have heard the National Anthem sung in almost every stadium where pro football is played. Every time I do a deep chill goes down my spine. A chill that flashes me back to the memory of a thatched hut that was built by the natives of Guam for a church after the Second World War.

The first services held there were led by an American chaplain, with a color guard ceremony performed by the marines. Just as the guards were about to raise the flag at the dedication of the church, an old lady, worn gray with age, hobbled bowlegged to the chaplain and asked if he would have her flag raised. As he nodded his head, she took out from a hidden pocket in her dress, an old American flag. She had kept it throughout the entire Japanese occupation of Guam. If she

had been caught she would have been imprisoned or executed. But now, on her own, she stood openly and proud as the flag was trumpeted into the sky.

From that day on, I started every game I officiated with tears in my eyes. No matter if I was in Green Bay, Philadelphia, Boston or Oakland, for me the lady from Guam was standing right there next to me.

The first thing the officials do after they get to the stadium is go into a series of pregame duties. The head linesman will go out early and talk to his chain crew. The field judge has a brief conference with the timekeeper. Officials will take a general look at the field to see if anything needs to be taken care of prior to play, to correct any unsafe conditions.

In the Astrodome the entire field consisted of two pieces of astroturf, joined in the middle by a Texas-style zipper. The turf can be put down and taken up to meet the needs of any given event. Once when I came in to work a game there, I noticed the yard lines that were zipped together were slightly askew. When I told the groundskeeper, he said, "If I don't fix that you could have a hell of an argument on your hands when they start to bring in the chains." He had it fixed, and flashed a big smile midway through the first quarter when one of the captains asked that we measure to make sure the other team had really made the first down. Now there's an important and thankless job. No public recognition in a spectacularly public place. Almost as invisible and thankless as the job of an official.

One hour before each game, an equipment manager brings twenty-four balls into the officials' dressing room. The referee checks them. He is the sole judge of their legality. They must be inflated to between 12½ and 13½ pounds.

With the advent of artificially lighted stadiums there was a problem with seeing the ball. That was solved by painting two stripes around the ball, one inch wide and about two and a half inches from each end. The pebble-grained leather has a "feel" to it which makes it easy to grip, but the painted strips were slippery. When the quarterback put his fingers on the laces and dropped his thumb over to the next panel (there are four panels on each ball) of leather, his thumb touched the painted stripe and his grip would slip.

In the sixties someone had a great idea. I am not sure but I've been told it was John Brodie, the San Francisco quarterback. He took a knife and scraped the stripe off the second panel to the left of the laces on each end of the ball. When he put the fingers of his right hand on the laces and dropped his thumb to the left he had bare leather. This eliminated the slipping.

The idea was such a good one that the league had the manufacturer make all night balls with the blank panels.

Later, when lefties Ken Stabler and Bobby Douglass made their ball clubs they put their left hand fingers on the laces and dropped their thumbs over to the right and there was that pesky stripe. So night balls were made with the stripes on the second panel to the right of the laces missing, and marked with "L" on the ball so we'd know it was for lefties.

After a couple of years the striping was modified to leave a small thumb space on all four sides. With improved lighting, the visibility has ceased to be a problem and all the stripes have been removed. Now the only stripes are on our shirts.

Some quarterbacks have asked us to let them get hold of the game ball before they get it into the game. This is in line with baseball umpires who rub up the balls to take the shine off them. I told one quarterback who kept pestering me about this to write the league office.

"I am not allowed to let you work with the ball until you get into the game. It's bad enough that they allow receivers to use "stick-um" glue on their hands to help them catch.

"Next thing you know, you guys will want to get some kind of 'completion jelly' in there and have your halfbacks use 'hand grip' so they won't fumble the ball."

"I didn't mean to upset you, ref. I just wanted to get used to the ball," the quarterback said.

During rainy and snow-driven games, just try pleasing quarterbacks and centers who want dry balls all the time. Every time you wipe off the mud and the rain, it comes back as soon as the ball is put down. We tried to remedy the situation by putting a towel on the ground but that didn't work. It got wet and players started tripping over it. Sometimes the umpire will stand with the ball and give it to the center as soon as he comes up to the line. I guess the best thing to do is offer some ideas for the all-through-the-game-dry ball, or the overhead stadium cover, for the constant dry touch.

It didn't matter to me what kind of turf a game was played on. The players had to fall on it. I wasn't suppose to. Knee injuries seemed to be somewhat reduced on synthetic surfaces, but the collision type injuries—the broken shoulders and split sternums increased. When it's raining the artificial turf is great. The mud in your whistle and in your eyes and inside your pants on the natural green sure is a mess.

Some of the ball clubs keep their balls from being kicked into the stands by raising a net behind the goal post. This isn't because they are cheap and don't want to lose them. They really aren't. They don't want to deny any kid having a souvenir. They just don't want anyone to get hurt.

A football at a big football game, especially the ball that was just in the game, is a tremendous 'attractive nuisance' for anyone. Especially the guy who ran clear across the stands after the touchdown to stand up there with his arms out waiting for the ball kicked for the extra point. The teams prevent any kind of hassle or harm among any of the fans with the net. If the ball gets into the stands though some clubs will have an usher come down and retrieve it. He will get the address of the 'receiver,' and tell him that the team will send him an autographed ball during the following week. People in the stands boo, when the usher comes to take the ball, but it's for everyone's safety.

The league is very consistent. A ball player who throws a ball into the stands to share and express his jubilation or upset is fined $150. Officials report the incident on their game cards, and a new ball is brought into the game.

In an All-Star game in the Oakland Coliseum we had some trouble. Down about the five yard line, up to about the fifteen, on one end of the field, there was a big puddle. It was deep enough that I was afraid some players would drown. And the last thing I wanted to do was give one of those big guys mouth-to-mouth when he's all full of fertilizer and mud.

We were coming up to the last part of the game when big, great big, Ernie Ladd—320, 6'11", 17½ EEEE shoes—walked over to me and said, "Hey, Big John. I lost my shoe." He's calling me big and I am talking to his navel.

"Where'd you put it?" I asked.

"It's in there somewhere."

"Oh, hell. Play without it. The game's almost over."

A couple of plays later we lost the football. There was a fumble, a big pileup, but no ball. I called time-out and started peeling guys off and when I got to the bottom I didn't have the ball.

"All right. Everyone show me your hands," I demanded. I thought they were trying to put something over on me, because it was only an All-Star game. There I was with the biggest kids in the world, trying to find out who was the bad boy.

I looked down and saw something with a lace going through it, and dug it out. I wasn't even sure it was the ball we were playing with. They asked whose ball it was and I said the West had it last and still has it. And on the next play Daryle Lamonica hit Rod Sherman with an eighty-two yard bomb for a touchdown.

Right before the kickoff is an anxious time. The teams are finishing their last minute instruction with their psyching-up hands-in-the-middle circles. Officials are refining their calm, intent upon making sure the show starts well. The fanfare of the opening whistle, the two teams coming at each other, the unedited edition of America's truth—Sunday readies itself for the most watched and scrutinized of national rites.

There have been both intentional and unintentional exceptions to the ceremonies running smoothly. Our crew was working a game in Houston when Pete Beathard was playing for the Oilers. Both Frank Kirkland, our field judge, and I knew Pete from his days as a player for the University of Southern California.

At the start of the game the Oilers were ready to kick-off. I was down under the receiver's goal post, getting ready to signal for the beginning of the game. I looked at each official for "his" ready signal—a raised hand over his head—but Frank was on the sideline in front of the Oilers' bench. He was talking on a phone. Just as I was going to signal the place kicker to wait, Frank angrily threw the phone down on the astroturf behind him. He then raised his hand, and I started the game.

At the first time-out, I asked him, "What the hell was going on with you and the telephone?" He said just as he was about to give me the "ready" signal, Pete Beathard tapped him on the shoulder with one of the field phones and said, "Telephone call from Long Beach, California, Frank."

Frank said, "I thought, my God, something terrible has happened at home and I grabbed the phone and said, 'Hello, hello, this is Frank Kirkland!!'"

The voice on the other end said, "Yes, we know. We can see you, Frank. This is the Oilers' scouting booth in the top of the stadium."

On the kickoff, the referee stands back with the receivers. I would usually ask them which way they were going to run, because, hell, I am going the other way.

I asked O.J. Simpson once, in the early years of his pro career, when he was running them back for Buffalo, which way he was going.

"I am going to the right and if I get a good block ten yards out I am going to cut across left and pick up the picket line and go all the way."

I said, incredulously, "If you go all the way, I'll buy you a milkshake." And by God, he did it. I told that story at a banquet in Riverside, California, and the headline writer put a headline on the story, NFL OFFICIAL BETS WITH BALLPLAYER. One of the owners of the Jets lived in Palm Springs and read the Riverside paper. I expected Mel Hein, the AFL Supervisor of Officials, to call me any minute, but he didn't.

Two words I try to avoid using together because it sounds so ugly are SHUT UP. However, in a football game they only sound semi-ugly. In keeping discipline on a bench and sidelines they sometimes work in controlling athletes, coaches, photo personnel and other team assistants.

The people I call the "extras," all those on the sidelines who aren't players or coaches, often think they have a better view of the action than the officials do and when they tell you about it they can get out of hand. I had a photographer come up to me when I was talking about a play with a captain and his coach, during a time-out and tell me that I was the blindest s.o.b. on the field. He said I could use his camera to watch the game.

He even offered me a pair of binoculars. I held up my index finger in his direction till I was through talking to the coach, then in as concise a way as I could, said, "Shut up and get back where you belong. And put that camera where it belongs."

Those two words came back to me. They were harsh but I don't feel anyone in the immediate vicinity doubted the necessity to use them. As I watched the guy back out of the players' section of the sidelines I couldn't help but think that he was hurt more by those two words than a player is after getting knocked around the field all day.

The referee has complete control of what happens on that field. He is in effect the complete policeman. He has to be. Another photographer, at a game I worked at San Bernardino's Orange Show Stadium, came onto the field after a touchdown was scored and screamed, "He didn't score! He didn't score! I got it on film. You can't score that TD, I got it on film!"

"What do you think this is, a horse race? Get off the

field. We don't use any photo finishes," I told him "gently."

He still wanted to argue. A cop was standing nearby and I waved him over. When he came I told him, "Take him clear out of the stadium. I mean clear out to the street."

As the officer was escorting him out he yelled back, "I am a newspaperman."

"Well you just lost the privilege of being inside. You should have been in the press box, anyway."

The old-time officials tell me that in the early days of pro football, it was a poor paying, part-time job for players and officials. Each team carried along its own "policeman," a player delegated to keep members of the other team from harming the men on his team. Any unsportsmanlike conduct, and the "officer" would exact comprehensive punishment on those who wronged. As far as I know there are no longer policemen in the game. We have taken their place, and the roughest we ever get is to separate the guys who are going to extremes with each other, and make sure disobedience is paid for with the loss of land, not limb.

You need a lot of fast retorts when players or coaches give you a hard time in their rapid critiquing of your work. Such compliments as:

"Hey, ref, why don't you get your head in the game?" and

"Straighten up, ref, you're missing a great game."

I usually ignore them or come back with a few one-liners like, "Why, thank you very much. I've had *good* football players (coaches) say the same thing," or "Gee, they thought it was a good call on the *other* bench." The safest comment of all, though, is to just tell them, "If they do the same thing, don't worry, I'll call it on them."

I never got too uptight when a player who had made a mistake—caused a foul—went around trying to lay the blame on someone else. I just figured he was out there looking out for his best interests. Of course, there was a limit to how much he could say and when he could say it. As a matter of fact, officials do them a favor by ignoring the verbal blasts. If we pay too much attention, we would wind up having to penalize them to regain game control.

Bob Austin, who was the first Supervisor of Officials in the American Football League, used to tell us that as long as a player calls you something in the heat of battle, nothing extreme and just between the two of you, it's up to you to come back with a fast answer and calm him down. You don't have to throw him out of the game or have to throw a flag on him. But if he starts to malign you out in front of the troops—the other players—and you feel you could lose game control, then you have to stop him with something that affects him and his team. Then the flag comes out.

Warnings to players about minor mistakes they are making can be done without causing any bias; in fact, players and coaches appreciate them. I am talking about someone who may be lining up a few inches offside, or be a tiny bit into the back edge of the ball. He can be warned, but only once. The next time he does it, he gets called for it.

You might see an official talking to a player on the field after a play and the official could be telling him, in reaction to the last play, "If you had grabbed him it would have been holding," or "If you had hit him you might not be in the game."

The clipping fouls, the striking fouls, anything unsportsmanlike, have to be called every time. One of the marks of a good official is if he can differentiate between the warning offenses and those that must always be called.

Let's say an umpire sees someone on offense who hasn't done anything wrong, yet, but he's starting to grab at people, so he's getting close to *Holding*. All that official has to say is, "Smith, keep your hands in." Right away it registers with Smith that, "he knows my name and he's watching." This kind of "preventive officiating" can help to keep the game from being spoiled by a lot of fouls. Calling out the player's name is effective for it makes the warning more direct and personal. The names on the backs of the players' jerseys is a great help in this department.

In pro football the guy you're playing against may have been your roommate last week. He may have been the guy you played with in high school or college. Two players pitted against each other might have been talked about in the press the preceding week. Players may even be bitter rivals, unprovoked by the news media. Whatever the circumstances, various discussion between and among the players on the field can and does go on.

Whenever the talk gets on the serious side an official can keep game control by moving in between plays and saying to the players involved, "Hey, let's knock off the chatter. This is a football game, not a debate."

What I used to do when it looked like it might turn into something more serious was to talk to the players individually. While the offensive team was in the huddle I'd call out the name of the defensive player—first or last name—and say, "Hey, Jim, he's getting to you. He's making you play his game. Don't let him get to you. Keep your cool," and walk away.

Then as I walked past the huddle or after the next play I would tell the offensive player the same thing.

Early in my career I was working a game at Fullerton Junior College, as head linesman. One of the players on the line started to move forward and was beginning to line up with his head clear into the ball and almost over the front edge of it, so I warned him.

"Number 58, back up, you're crowding the ball."

So he backed up for two or three plays following, but on the next play he lined up way forward again. When the ball was snapped I threw the flag on him, went and reported the foul to the referee who then walked off the five yards against his team.

The player's coach yelled at me, "Who was offside? Who was offside?"

"Number 58." I told him.

"You're supposed to warn him once," he hollered back to me.

The kid in the huddle heard this and he straightened up and looked over to his coach and yelled to him, "He warned me, coach—he warned me."

I thought the coach was going to die laughing. I turned around and he was actually on the ground roaring. He looked at me and said, "You better quit while you're ahead. You may never get a guy to do something like that again."

And he was right. It's never happened since.

When players complain to officials that another player is shoving them or pushing off on them officials will usually say, "I'll take a look."

Officials tend to respect players who don't have the reputation for being criers. Usually if a player sees the man he is playing against go over to an official and it looks like he is complaining, it's almost certain that for the next couple of plays he won't do whatever it may be that he is being accused of. Players might feel that after they complain about another player that the official will devote all of his attention to that player, but that's not how it works.

The official has specific places that his mechanics direct him to look. The mechanics determine the areas he has to concentrate on and he can't spend all of his energies looking at one player until he catches him in the act.

Sometimes players will unknowingly cause another player to stop fouling them. One instance of this happened with Ben Agajanian. Ben is one of those guys, who like George Blanda, goes on forever. He was a place-kicker for about half the teams in professional football.

I got to know him before I went into officiating in the pros, when he owned a sporting goods store in Santa Ana. When the AFL was born he became the kicker for the Los Angeles (now the San Diego) Chargers. On September 10, 1960, they played the Dallas Texans (now the Chiefs of

Kansas City) in the Los Angeles Coliseum. Dallas had a player on its specialty units whose job was to wait for Ben when he came downfield. On one kick just prior to the half, he threw a block that cracked one of Ben's fingers.

When Ben came out for the second half kickoff he walked over to me. He put one of his arms around me, held out his injured hand and said, "Hey, old buddy, take a look at this and watch that guy down there." He pointed to the damaging player.

"Don't put your arm around me. We're on television, and the commissioner doesn't like to see any kind of affection shown between players and officials."

Ben looked at me surprised and moaned, "How can you treat me like that?"

"It's easy, Ben. When I referee, I swear off all friendships for a few hours. He laughed and walked away, but the scene got the desired result. The Dallas player saw us and left Ben alone for the rest of the game.

The New York Giants and the Boston Patriots were playing in the Yale Bowl on October 18, 1970. Fran Tarkenton, who was the quarterback for the Giants then, had another habit besides scrambling around the backfield. He would stand with me near the ball and wait until I started the thirty second count before he went into the huddle to call his signals. No other quarterback that I knew of did this. He probably didn't want any help from his teammates in selecting a play.

He was playing in this game when all of a sudden a couple of fans got into a fight. The crowd pulled back to give the fighters room, and Boston's "finest" couldn't get to them. Everyone was watching them. Even the players on the field. Tarkenton looked at me and said, "What's going on?"

"There's a fight up there." Just as he said it one of the guys knocked the other over about four rows of seats.

Fran said, "Wow, that's a hell of a fight."

I said, "Come on, Fran, we got a football game to play."

"What do you mean? The fight's better than the game."

He was right.

About the middle of the first quarter, while I was working an Oiler game in Houston's Jeppison Stadium there was a fight between two players. We kicked the two pugilists out of the ball game.

Later, towards the middle of the second quarter, there was another fight. I heard a player who was running in from the bench yell, "Let me take a shot at him. I've already been kicked out of the game."

I recognized the voice and took a quick look at my game card, and there it was. Number 78 was an ejectee from the earlier fight.

I grabbed him by the arm, and whirled him around and said, "Hey, friend, you're not only out of the game, you're out of the stadium—head for the showers and don't come back."

As he was leaving he turned and smiled and said, "Thanks a lot, ref. I got an early date, anyway."

In the Minnesota-San Diego preseason game of 1971 both benches emptied onto the field to join in the fighting and each player was assessed a healthy fine by the commissioner for leaving the bench and getting into the melee. The fines, however, were subsequently dropped and the monies returned to the players because the league had never bargained with the Players' Association concerning the invoking of a fine for coming off the bench to join in a fight.

The year after I retired, I ran into Bum Phillips, who at the time of the fight was an assistant coach of the San Diego Chargers, and is now the Head Coach of the Houston Oilers. While we were having lunch, Bum told me that the San Diego owner had paid the fines for his players and later when the league returned the fines to each player, according to the court order, only one or two players sent their fine back to the owner. So, in effect, each San Diego player got a bonus for getting into a fight.

I remember another fight where both benches emptied onto the field. Both benches were on the same side of the field. The game film zeroed in on two guys who were running towards the fight, one from each bench. One of them had his helmet on and the other one didn't. The one with his helmet on turned toward the other guy and yelled and the guy with his helmet off laughed and put his helmet on, and they both ran to the edge of the fight and started pushing each other. They were probably former roommates before one or both of them got traded. One thing a player should remember is, "Never take your helmet off in a fight."

My friend, Ben Drieth of Denver, Colorado, is a referee now and used to be our field judge. When I say he was our field judge, I am referring to when he was on our crew. He's a college basketball referee in the off-season, and when he calls a penalty he really lets a player have it. He throws that flag down and points to the player and yells accusingly, "You, 84!! You clipped him!!"

I used to say to him, "Hey, Ben, the guy never clipped you or bit you. You don't have to get so mad at him," but he'd always act it out that way. That's Ben's style, and he's one of the best in the business. When Ben's refereeing there is no doubt about who's in control.

My style was different. I've kissed the Blarney Stone and I'm Irish so I'd try to needle the players by appealing to their pride as pros. Let me give you an example. A young rookie came up to the pros from college weighing about 280 pounds. He was playing for the Denver Broncos and on this day was up against the San Francisco 49ers. His position was opposite an old veteran by the name of Woodrow (Woody) Peoples.

Because he was so big, he probably got away with a lot

of "crying" to officials when he was in college. And the college officials, because they saw a guy like him maybe only once in a season, would start paying attention to whatever he would complain about. Well, he was up there now with a lot of guys who were as big or almost as big as he was and he started crying to me in a low whisper, "He's holding me. He's holding me."

He kept saying this to me and I started thinking to myself, "I'd better straighten this rookie out, right now," and so I asked him, "Who's holding you, sonny?"

"Number 69. Right there. Number 69," and pointed to Woody who was getting up to go back to his huddle.

So I said, "Hey rookie, you mean that little guy? Why he only weighs about 225 pounds. If I was as big as you I wouldn't let him hold me back in the least. I'd go by him so fast, it'd bust his arm."

He gave me a dirty look, and as he walked by the 49er huddle, he pointed at Peoples, and said, "You hold me on the next play and I'll bust you right in the mouth."

I hollered, "You better do it legal, son." He looked over to me in a mild glare as the 49ers got into their huddle. When they broke and came into their positions on the line I noticed something was a slight bit different. Woody Peoples had shifted to the other side of the center. I figured something's up so I backed up another five or six yards 'cause I didn't want to end up underneath it.

The play broke and the guy playing opposite the rookie flared out for the outside linebacker leaving a great big hole right in the middle of the line and standing back there—just messing around with the football—was the man with the golden arm, San Francisco quarterback, John Brodie. The rookie's eyes lit up like fifty-cent pieces. And Woody, unknown to the rookie, was just waiting over there for him to come after Brodie. When he did Woody stepped around the center and stuck his headgear right square in the rookie's middle, flipped him into a complete somersault and he landed spread-eagled right down in front of me.

I looked down at him and said, "I suppose you're gonna tell me he held you on that play?"

He never said another word the rest of the game and I think he went on to be one of the best rookies that year.

The strangest football-crying story I know, didn't involve a player or a coach, but of all people, an owner. Harry Wismer was the first owner of the New York Titans, the team that became the New York Jets in 1963, when Sonny Werblin and his four associates purchased the franchise for $1,000,000.

On September 16, 1962, the Titans played the Chargers in San Diego. Harry Wismer was on the sidelines following the line of scrimmage up and down the field. A few plays before the end of the half, Titan quarterback Lee Grosscup was running along his own eight yard line looking for a receiver. He was holding the ball, ready to pass, when 260-pound Earl Faison blind-sided him. The ball popped out and went forward from one of the most devastating blows I have ever seen in football. It was a fumble, pure and simple, because Grosscup had not started his passing motion. One of the Chargers picked up the ball and ran it into the end zone for a touchdown.

Harry Wismer came unglued. He stomped and kicked everything near him, but had the good sense to stay off the field. As soon as the half was over, Wismer came charging up to me, screaming. "That was an incomplete pass and you called it a fumble."

I told him in my usual calm manner, "That play will be called a fumble, today, tomorrow, and next year, by every referee in the league."

"You gave them a gift touchdown. That was the turning point in the game."

I don't think anyone, including the Titan team, would have agreed with him, because that touchdown made the score about 30 to 7, in favor of the Chargers. (The final score was 40-14). I told him that if he came down to the dressing room area we could continue the conversation.

When we got there he yelled at me, "You robbed us and you'll never work a game in this league again."

"Maybe not, Mr. Wismer, but I am working this one. And, if you're on the sidelines the second half, I'll forfeit the game to San Diego."

"You can't do that," he exploded. "I own this club. You can't do that to me."

"You may own that ball club but I am running the football game, and I don't want to see you on the sidelines the second half. And if you want to wait a minute, I'll go get my rule book out and show you where it says I can forfeit the game."

He glowered at me and walked into the Titan dressing room. He wasn't on the sidelines during the second half. About half way through the third quarter, I glanced up at the press box during a time-out, and there he was.

When the game was over I headed for the nearest telephone and reported the incident to the supervisor of officials. He assured me that the league commissioner, Joe Foss, would take care of the situation.

The next week in Oakland when the officials came onto the field, Joe Foss was waiting for me. We shook hands and he told me, "I took care of Harry Wismer for you, John. I screwed his hat on real tight."

"What'd you do to him, skipper?" I asked.

"Well," he said. "He is no longer allowed on the sidelines in any American Football League game. I also fined him a dollar for every step it took him to get from the field to the press box in San Diego's stadium." I've often wanted to pace it off to find out how much it cost Mr. Wismer to make that expensive trip.

In 1960 my family and I were driving to the Los Angeles Coliseum where I was to referee a Charger game. Beth, who was a choir director, explained to me that an anthem should be a participatory thing and people were supposed to stand and sing the national anthem, not stand there like posts while someone else sang. She suggested that the public address announcer should ask the people to join in the singing.

When the Coliseum public address announcer, John Ramsey came into our dressing room prior to the game I told him what Beth said. That night he said, "Ladies and gentlemen will you please rise and join our soloist in singing our national anthem."

I don't know if John Ramsey is the first public address announcer to do this but I believe he started the custom. John is the voice in almost every professional sports team in Los Angeles so he has probably asked more people to stand and honor their country than any man alive.

When a dignitary is in the stands, and notice is made by the public address, almost anything can happen. Fans can get into a frenzy, and even officials occasionally lose their composure.

When Richard Nixon was president, he attended a game in Miami between the Dolphins and the Oakland Raiders. The Air Force had sent out its finest band and color guard in full dress uniforms, to play *The Star-Spangled Banner*. After they finished playing I looked at my officials for their signal. Frank Kirkland was taking the ball out on the field to give to the kicker. Then he ran over to the sidelines and raised his "ready" hand. I blew the whistle and the kickoff began.

At the first time-out, Frank came up to me and said, "Man, Big John. You're really patriotic, aren't you?"

"What are you talking about?"

"You couldn't wait, could you? You ran the entire Miami football team right through the color guard."

"Oh, my God!" You should have seen the game pictures the following week at our pregame meeting. The color guard was up on their tip toes and sprinting delicately off the field.

Tommy Miller, my line judge that day, was the guy who fired the gun at the end of each quarter. At a time-out near the end of the second quarter I told him to look up at the president.

"Do you see all the guys in the black suits around him?"

"Yeah," Tommy said. "Looks like the Mafia."

"For Chrissakes, when you fire the gun don't aim it towards them 'cause they'll drill you right through the heart."

Sure enough, when the quarter was over Tommy turned his back on the president, and instead of firing the gun into the air, aimed it towards the ground and fired.

At halftime he told me "I took one look at those guys and decided not to take any chances. They look like they could drill you right through the heart."

SIX

I loved it.
Every minute of it.
The conflict.
The battle of wits.

Anybody can call an offside foul. A guy jumps offside and the whole place sees it. No sweat. Some calls are even more obvious. Once a lineman stripped the headgear off a ball carrier. I penalized him fifteen yards for grabbing the face mask. Some face mask fouls only get a five yard penalty. The yardage depends on how flagrant it is.

In this particular play the helmet and headgear were torn clear off and when the yardage was marched off, the coach screamed at me as if I was being unfairly harsh for charging the total fifteen. I just lifted the arm of the player who made the foul, who was in a daze as he looked over at the coach, the telltale helmet still in his hand. When I pointed to the runner nearby who was busy massaging his ears as he looked for his helmet, the coach then laughed.

The way you really earn your money though is when you've got to make the tight, tough ones—the ones where eighty to a hundred million people might be watching and ready to tell you unmercifully that you're wrong.

Atlanta was playing in Cincinnati in the preseason, and Cincinnati's coach was Paul Brown, the supreme dean of coaching. At that time about half of the head coaches in the league had been his assistants or had played for him. Nobody likes anything better than to beat the teacher. One of those guys was Norm "Dutch" Van Brocklin, who was coaching the Atlanta Falcons that day. The score was 14 to 14 coming into the end of the first half. And right in front of the Cincinnati bench, Atlanta fumbled and Cincinnati recovered. Now,

Paul Brown is one of those coaches who knows the rule book forwards and backwards. There's a rule in pro football that says substitutes always have to go off on their own side of the field. Well this kid's a rookie in the preseason, and he steps off right in front of the Cincinnati team and goes into their bench area. Paul Brown got in front of him, hiding him. Later we found out he was patting him on the stomach telling him how great he's been. And the kid's standing there thinking, "The great Paul Brown thinks I'm super."

So the Bengals send in the field goal team and they go to kick the field goal and miss it. When they kick it, the clock turns up double zero and the half should be over, but I hear this high-pitched voice over there saying, "Mac, hey Mac!" Only one guy in the whole league ever called me Mac and that's Paul Brown, and now he's patting this guy right on the chest and he says "Look what I got here."

This rookie is off the field on the wrong side and Paul Brown knows the rule that if the defense fouls in the last time down in the half, the offense gets the penalty plus one untimed down free of foul by the defense. The guy off the field on the wrong side is a defensive foul.

I said, "Oh God," and threw the flag up and told the kid, "Get over on your own side!"

I sneaked a look at Van Brocklin and he's just turning livid. So we move the ball up five yards and they try it again and they miss it again but this time their left end is offside and the head linesman gets him. Now Van Brocklin's about to go nuts and move it up five more yards. They're getting in range now. They try it again, they miss it again and this time the left end lands right on top of the holder. It says right there in the book, "Thou shalt not land on the holder" and I had to nail him. Now, we're really up there close and Van Brocklin's about to go up like a skyrocket. So they try it again and the Falcons block it and the half is over. When I looked over there three assistants and my umpire are trying to keep him from coming after me. Thank God they stopped him!!

It's at times like that that you earn your money. It turned out that by the end of the game Van Brocklin was leading by about thirty points. When I went over to give him the two minute warning he saw me coming and said, "Yeah, okay John, two minutes. Tell your guys they worked a great game tonight." It sure makes a difference when you're ahead. I always liked "Dutch"; his teams were well coached and they never gave up.

I remember one time when Atlanta was playing the Rams and Deacon Jones was the Los Angeles captain. There was a foul against the Falcons just before halftime and the Deacon came over to me and asked, "What have you got, sweetheart?"

I told him there was a clipping foul and what the options were and he took the penalty. When the half was over and we were all walking up the tunnel, Van Brocklin came up behind me and said, "Hey, John, how come you let that guy call you sweetheart?"

"Well, if you're 6'5" tall and weigh 260 pounds you can call me any name you want, but you're not so you don't have to think about calling me anything out of line, all right?" We both looked at each other and started to laugh.

Another time I earned my money well was on Sunday, October 1, 1972, when the Washington Redskins were playing the New England Patriots in Foxboro, Massachusetts. Up until this time in the season the Redskins hadn't lost a game and the Patriots had won one and lost one. It came down to the end of the game with about 1:03 left on the clock and Washington kicked a field goal to tie the score at 24 to 24. Unfortunately, a Patriot end ran into the kicker so I threw a flag on him and everybody in Boston was ready to hang me. Now the 'Skins' had a choice. They could leave it 24-24 and take the penalty on the next kick-off or they could set the score back to 21-24, take the penalty which would give them a first down on the eighteen yard line. The strategy is that they can run three plays and if they don't score a touchdown they can still kick a field goal and tie it up again.

George Allen, the Redskins' coach, made the only choice he really had and the Redskins set the score back to 21-24 and took possession. Well, they ran three plays and missed the field goal attempt. There were about thirty seconds left on the clock, and in came the offensive team from Boston. We put the ball on the twenty because a missed field goal from inside the twenty is a touchback. The Pats had the ball first and ten on the twenty going out. Jim Plunkett, who played at Stanford with my son, came running by me and said, "That's the greatest call you ever made, John."

"Yeah, but they didn't think so a few minutes ago."

The Pats ran three plays and didn't make their first down. There were four seconds left on the clock and they had to kick. The 'Skins blocked the kick and the ball rolled across the end zone. Just as it rolled out the guy that blocked it tried to fall on it. He never really controlled it but he rolled over the top of it and out of bounds. But, a split second before he fell on the ball, his own end came sliding in on the wet surface to scoop it in. He touched the football just as both of his feet were touching the end line. The rule says that a loose ball touched by a player or anything else, in contact with, or outside of a boundary line is immediately dead and out of bounds. As he touched the ball he was out of bounds, which made the ball out of bounds. He caused it to be out of bounds and it was a two point safety for Washington making it 24-23 ending in favor of New England. I gave the signal for a safety—both palms together over my head—and moved President Nixon off the front page of the Washington Post for the whole week.

Every time a flag is thrown, keep your eyes on the official that called the foul. Watch him closely and you will see him report this foul to the referee and then take a card out of his own pocket and write on it. He's writing the time on the clock, the quarter, the foul, the number of the player who committed the foul, and if possible, the man he fouled; whether it was on the offense or defense, whether it was accepted, rejected or offset and how many other officials called it. After the game, each official takes a 5''x 7'' card and lists all the fouls he called and other information and gives it to the referee. The referee will have seven cards like that, his and six others, and a tally card that he makes out for an entire report on the ball game. If a player is ejected from the game a special report (it will be a legal document) has to go in because the league is going to separate the player from some of his money. All this goes in an envelope which is sent special delivery to the league office the minute the referee gets to the airport after the game.

In the stands is a retired official, an observer, who makes another report on the officiating. In the press box, in all big games, college and pro, there's a guy who knows football like you can't believe and can type like mad. He types out the entire game on a ditto stencil. Every time the ball changes hands he slips in a red one and then pulls it out so it becomes purple, red, purple, red, as the ball changes hands. He puts every play down. For instance, it might say 1-10, D-36, (first and ten on the Dallas thirty-six), Staubach throws to so and so, etc. At the end of each quarter this is run off on a ditto machine and runners take it all through the press box. This is why at half time you might hear an interview with an announcer who says "In the third play of the first quarter the quarterback threw a short pass and . . ." You think the guy's got a hell of a memory when he's just reading it off a paper.

At the end of the game the observer gets these reports, puts them with his own report and sends them to the league office immediately. Within a few hours after the game, a copy of the film is on its way to New York, with every play in slow motion. On Monday, I would call New

York and give them a verbal report on the game. By Wednesday the film, and reports are in the league office in New York. The supervisors look at every play of every game in the National Football League and they check every call. Anything they thought you missed is all written on that ditto that was run off up in the press box. All of it goes into a film package and is sent air express to the hotel where that officiating crew will be next week. When the crew gets there on Saturday, they spend two to three hours looking at the films for self-improvement and to help them answer any of those probing questions the supervisors ask.

In the game situation the official calling a foul would run to me and tell me the foul:

"I've got clipping on Red number fifty-six on the thirty yard line." They tell me what, who and where, and then stay near me until I interpret this for the captain or captains of the teams, and to be sure there is no misunderstanding.

Consider clipping—which used to be a twenty-five yard penalty—now it's fifteen. Clipping by the offense is penalized from the spot of the clipping if it occurred behind the end of the run. If it occurred beyond the end of the run it would be penalized from the end of the run. If it occurred after the runner had gone out of bounds it would go from where he crossed the sideline.

A clip is what you call a "spot" foul. An official must throw his flag down at the spot where the infraction occurred. The chances are he's calling one of two things, either defensive pass interference or a clipping foul. The spot where the flag lands or where he adjusts the flag on the ground is where the penalty may or may not be stepped off. Of course, if there's pass interference on the defense, the offense is awarded the ball right at the spot of the thrown flag with first and ten.

For those of you who run to the hot dog lines, to get there first and miss the last minute of the second quarter, for those of you who don't stay 'til the end of the game because it's quicker to get on the freeway than staying to the end of the game, or as an armchair official, there is one rule you don't get to see implemented.

If the offense fouls on the last play of a half—the clock runs out—no points scored will count. If the offense runs the ball and they score a touchdown but there is an offensive clip on the play, the game is over, there is no penalty and the touchdown does not count.

Suppose the offense starts to run with the ball and there is a holding foul by the defense and the offense doesn't score. The offense will then get an extra down, free of a foul by the defense. If the defense fouls again, the offense will get another play. The game is extended until the offense gets one play without a foul being committed by the defense.

If the offense throws a pass on the last play of the game and the defense intercepts it and in their return of the ball they are fouled by the "now" defensive team, they will get another play from scrimmage, even though the clock has run out and the game would normally be over. The defensive team at the beginning of the play was the offensive team when the foul was committed and therefore is treated with offensive rights. This one thing gives rookie high school officials more trouble than almost anything else.

We had a situation at the end of a high school game in Santa Ana a few years ago. The score was 21-20 in favor of the visiting team and the home team kicked a field goal from the five yard line as the clock hit zero. However, there was a flag down because the home team had five men in the backfield and six on the line. The rule says you must have seven men on the line when you are on offense. The kick was good but the young referee thought, "They can't score when they foul, " so he gave the options to the defensive captain, telling him, "You can take the penalty and they will have another down after a five yard penalty, or you can let the play stand and they win 23-21."

Naturally the captain chose to make them run another

down after the five yard penalty. They kicked another field goal and won the game. Everyone picked up their gear, shook hands, sang their respective "Alma Maters" and went home.

Sounds logical, doesn't it?

Well, when I read the papers the next morning I figured I'd be getting a flock of telephone calls about it. No one has called me yet.

What was wrong was that the rookie official didn't completely understand the rule which states, "If the offense fouls on the last timed down of the game, the game is over, and *no points scored will count.*" Only when the defense fouls on the last play, do you extend the half until the offense gets one play free of a foul by the defense.

According to their league rules, one of the schools would have to file an appeal before I could make any sort of ruling. Obviously none of the coaches knew the rule either. There is an old saying, "Never trouble trouble, trouble will find you if it wants you."

I had a similar play a number of years ago in Denver that caused a problem, probably because the Denver fans, who were new to pro football, didn't understand the rule.

The Kansas City Chiefs were playing the Denver Broncos. Kansas City scored just before the half to put them within three points of the Broncos. Four seconds were left in the half when they kicked off to the Broncos. It was an onside kick and a Kansas City player recovered it. He could not advance it because his team kicked it.

By rule, the clock did not start when Kansas City legally recovered their own kick. A league rule at that time was that during the last two minutes of a half, the clock didn't start after a kickoff until the referee signalled, "ready for play." The rule has since been changed so that the clock starts on the snap of the ball. One of the Denver players, I believe it was the middle guard, smacked through the line just after I put the ball in play, causing a five yard penalty for encroachment, just as the clock ran down to zero. I marked off the penalty. Because it was a defensive foul on the last down of the half, Kansas City got an extra play. And, on that play Kansas City kicked a field goal, right through the uprights. Denver fans went wild as the scoreboard showed no time left and the game tied.

A Denver sportswriter was outside the official's dressing room along with league commissioner, Joe Foss. Joe gave me permission to talk with the writer who wanted me to explain what had happened; how time is handled in the last two minutes, and other advice I could give him on how to calm down an irate populace who thought they had their victory given away by a bad or fast call. Not too many people, it seemed, were aware that the clock didn't start when a team legally recovered its own kick, and that a foul by the defense, when time runs out on a play, automatically gives the offense another play, free of a foul by the defense.

I'll bet ninety-nine percent of the seasoned followers of the "Orange Crush" wouldn't be fooled by that rule today, thanks to that Denver writer.

I don't blame fans, players, and coaches for sometimes becoming confused on the playing rules of football. Between college and pro ball there are about a hundred and twenty differences in the rules. There are only about thirty differences between the pro and high school rules. One of the obvious college and pro differences is the time allowed to put the ball into play. It's thirty seconds in pro, and twenty-five seconds in college.

When you're watching a pass play that is ending near the out-of-bounds lines, in college, the receiver only has to have one foot inbounds after he has possession of the ball for the pass to be declared complete. In the pro ranks, both feet of the receiver must touch inbounds before a pass is complete. The chalk lines are *out of bounds,* and if a player touches them *he* is out of bounds.

There are about a hundred and fifty differences between the National Federation High School rules and the National Collegiate Athletic Association laws of play, so don't be too hard on a kid going from high school to college when he "blows" one once in a while.

In the beginning of the AFL, Buffalo was playing Houston. Buffalo had a chance to make the playoffs. Houston didn't. We were going into the closing minutes of the game and Buffalo was ahead by a few points and had possession of the ball near the Houston twenty-five yard line. It was third down with a few yards to go. They had come out of the huddle and I had started the thirty second count with the field judge. The quarterback started calling signals and all of the sudden the field judge blew his whistle, threw his flag in the air, and gave the signal for "delay," which meant they had exceeded the thirty second count. Now on a delay foul you don't need to ask the captain, you just pick up the ball, walk off the five yards, give the signal, and get on with the game. As I leaned over to pick up the ball, I glanced at the clock behind me and saw 1:58 left in the game, which meant one of two things:

1. The field judge did not stop the game at two minutes because he was thinking of the thirty second count, or
2. The timekeeper had let the clock slide over a few seconds and the thirty seconds was up at say 2:01 or 2:02.

I asked the field judge if he was sure it was for delay and he yelled back to me, "Delay! Delay!" So I marched off the five yards, then gave the teams the two minute warning.

Buffalo went back into the huddle, probably changed their strategy and came out with a pass play. It was intercepted. Houston took over with that old retreaded quarterback who everybody thought was over the hill, George Blanda. He took his team down with passes

    zip ----- out of bounds
    zip ----- out of bounds
    time out
    zip ----- out of bounds

He moved his team to the other end of the field, hit a receiver in the end zone and scored with just a few seconds left and won.

After the game the field judge came into the dressing room and told me he blew the foul, that he should have called time out for the two minute warning and not delay of the game. Ralph Wilson, the owner of the Bills, went right through the roof, and rightly so.

The next morning I got a call from Thurlo McCrady, supervisor of officials, who wanted to know what had happened. I explained it to him and then wrote out a report which stated that one of the prime duties of the field judge was to keep the time, that I had checked with him and that a mistake had definitely been made.

I suffered with this whole thing for a week. The media got hold of it. One writer for the Los Angeles Times even closed one of his columns by saying that it looked as if five officials would loose their stripes. To make things worse I had the next weekend off. During the broadcast of a game that Sunday, and announcer said on television that Buffalo owner Ralph Wilson had demanded that all officials of the Buffalo-Houston game be fired.

That would do it. I figured I was on my way out. The next day, I got a call from Thurlo and he said there would be some fines levied and that the field judge was no longer in the league. I got a letter from commissioner Joe Foss, and sent in a $125 fine. As luck would have it, I was assigned the Buffalo-Denver game for the following Sunday.

The Denver stadium had two clocks and the only one that Buffalo could see malfunctioned. The Buffalo coach yelled at me about it. I stopped the game to find out from the timer what was wrong. He told me that the clock couldn't be fixed.

I told the coach that we would tell him the official time remaining in the game after each play. "It will come from the head linesman, who is right in front of you. We'll yell it to him and he'll yell it to you."

I found out later that Mr. Wilson had called Thurlo the following day to tell him what a fine job he thought the referee did in improvising through the broken clock situation. Thurlo told him I was the same referee who had worked the game two weeks before.

All the guys on the crew thought the fine wasn't fair but none of them thought enough about it to kick in some money to help me pay it.

Late in the season the incident turned a full circle. After one of the postseason play-off games, Joe Foss came up to me. When he shook my hand I felt some paper. At first I thought it was notice that I wouldn't be working in the league for the following year. Not quite. It was the money I had paid for the fine. So far as I have been able to find out no other official has ever been fined but they have been suspended. When you're suspended from a game or two, though for a mistake, it's the same as being fined.

I made a mistake once by taking something for granted. After every score, the referee must ask the captain of the team scored upon if he wants to kick or receive. One in a thousand times, on a windy, rainy day, he might decide to kick. This caused me some embarrassment once at Balboa Stadium in San Diego.

The captain of the scored-upon team said, "We'll take the wind and kick off," and then ran to his bench.

As soon as the kicking team kicked the extra point I turned and ran to the far end of the field to get ready for the kickoff. When I got there I turned around and there were the two teams lined up ready to kick off, and I suddenly realized that I should be at the other end of the field, one hundred yards away, under the receiving team's goal post. Instead, there I was thirty yards behind the kicking team, looking at their backs.

I didn't dare blow the whistle because the kicker would kick off. Instead, I yelled, "Wait a minute." He turned and gave me a puzzled look as I ran by him.

"Don't kick the ball until I signal you from the other end of the field."

The stadium was filled and there was a large TV audience, not to mention the incredulous members of my crew. Everyone waited while I ran a one hundred yard solo all the way down to the other end of the field. As a cover-up to those who might have asked questions about what I was doing, I first ran over to the TV coordinator on the sidelines to make it look like the delay was caused by television.

I even acted out the part asking him, "Are you ready?"

Surprised, he answered, "We've been ready for quite a while, John." I sprinted down to stand under the goal post and then signaled for the kickoff.

After the game, my boss, Thurlo McCrady, said, "You were really busy checking things out down there before that kickoff. What was the delay for?" I earned most of the money I got paid that day 'talking' myself off the hook.

I am not saying that officials don't miss calls or make some errors in officiating mechanics. I will always remember though what I heard the late coach Red Sanders of UCLA say after a game I officiated. He answered a question from a reporter who asked his feelings about the officiating of the game and with his very droll sense of humor he said, "Well, gentlemen, I'll tell ya. There's three elements in a ball game. There's the players and there's the coaches and there's the officials. And, if I can ever get my players and my coaches to make as few mistakes as the officials, there ain't nobody who's ever going to beat us. Any more questions?"

SEVEN

*We've proven to officials we don't love
the human element, we don't excuse
their mistakes and won't let them re-
pent.*

from Super Fans by Paul T. Owens

Any official who tells me he's never blown an inadvertent
whistle is either lying, fooling himself, or both. I'm not sure
I want him working with me because he apparently doesn't
have the in-depth knowledge, or feel for the game that will
keep him constantly alert to blowing one. One of the last
things I said in every final pregame conference was,
"Remember, don't hit your whistle unless you actually see
the ball become dead in the possession of the player."

Instant replays can help in some situations, but not with an
inadvertent whistle. The replay will show you what happened
after the whistle, but by the dictates of the rule book, that action has no bearing on the play because everything that happens after the whistle sounded is on a dead ball, the play has

ILLEGAL FORWARD PASS

ended. If human beings didn't blow whistles that stop plays, all the players would run the risk of very serious injury. There is no machine capable of following the moves of a wide receiver, that can signal the other twenty-one players, "The ball is dead, stop the action."

Right now, Rule 7, Section 4, Article 1, of the NFL rule book covers the fifteen ways in which a ball becomes dead and the down is ended. Paragraph (n) states:

"When any official signals dead ball or sounds his whistle, even though *inadvertently,* the ball is dead."

I think most owners and coaches, when they stop and really think about it, would tell you that they would much rather have a rare inadvertent whistle than a busted up ball player.

Suffice it to say, that the official who blows an unintentional whistle feels as rotten about it as a receiver feels about the pass that he dropped in the end zone, or as badly as the field goal kicker feels about the second straight game-losing kick he missed. The player has many chances to redeem himself, but the official who blows an inadvertent whistle must live with the horror of it for the rest of his life.

There are basically two types of inadvertent whistles. One occurs when the quarterback fakes so well that he not only fools the defense, but the officials as well. The whistle is blown on the faker instead of the taker. But no matter how far the runner gets, the ball is dead where the ball was when the whistle was blown. It's a left-handed compliment to the quarterback for keeping everybody in the dark, except for his teammates. With seven officials in the pro ranks, this type of inadvertent whistle rarely occurs.

The second type of misblown whistle is the one that is sounded after the ball is fumbled.

We went back to work a game between Atlanta and Minnesota in Bloomington on November 28, 1972. It was just before halftime and Minnesota had the ball on Atlanta's seven or eight yard line. The next play Minnesota opened a wide gap and went straight through to score a touchdown. On that play, just as the guy with the ball crossed the five yard line a whistle sounded. Right away I am thinking one of my guys blew an inadvertent whistle. I looked at my officials and they all looked stunned. Harry Kessel, our head linesman, was signalling "touchdown" when I suddenly realized what had happened. A high school band was standing there ready to go on the field for the halftime entertainment. I figured immediately that the drum major had hit his whistle to bring his band to attention. I ran straight up to him, grabbed his whistle in my hand, shook my finger in his face and told him, "Don't you blow this thing again 'til halftime." His eyes popped out like ping pong balls. "Yes sir! Yes sir!"

I ran back onto the field and as I passed one of the Atlanta players, he said, "Hey, one of your guys blew a whistle."

"No, he didn't. It was the drum major of that band."

"Okay," he said. Thank God I saw the kid and the whistle and connected them together; otherwise we could have had a protest that looked like a filibuster in the United States Senate. Nothing can cause more problems to both teams than for somebody to get a whistle and bring it to the game and start making their own game calls. This can really hurt the game and particularly the players.

Once we were down in San Diego, and deep into the third quarter when this self-appointed official started blowing his whistle in the middle of every play when the visiting team had the ball. It confused the hell out of everybody. Captains were complaining and finally I just stopped the clock. I went over to the sideline phones and called the public address announcer and told him to announce that both captains have requested that the person blowing the whistle in the stands please refrain from doing so, as it is confusing to both teams. The public address announcer spoke out abruptly, "Your attention please! The referee has ordered that the person in the stands blowing the whistle stop blowing it or he will penalize San Diego." The entire place suddenly sounded like Birdland, U.S.A. People must have gone out and bought whistles and brought them in. It was chaos for the rest of the game.

A few weeks later at another game, there was a similar situation. A fan in the stands started blowing a whistle, just before the half. When we went down to the officials' dressing room at halftime I telephoned up to the press box and asked to speak to the public address announcer. When he got on the phone, I said, "Now, I am going to tell you something. I want you to write it down and I want you to read it exactly as I have give it to you. I don't want you to add or take away one word." He agreed.

"What do you want me to say?"

"I want you to say, 'Your attention, please. Someone in the stands is blowing a whistle. It is confusing both football teams and it is a dangerous thing to do. The captains and the coaches of both teams have requested that you do not blow the whistle any more. We would appreciate your consideration for everybody on the field. Thank you.'"

I told him not to say anything else and above all not to threaten them. As soon as we came onto the field for the second half the announcer read it exactly as I said and we never heard another whistle out of the crowd. The first way was done with a threat and no one in a crowd wants to abide by that. The second way was by request of the players and coaches and everyone seemed to respect it. If the guy who blew the whistle had done it again I think the people around him would have clobbered him good.

If you invite Rosey Gilhousen, the famed baseball scout, to speak at your banquet, there's a good chance that he'll tell you the story of when he worked a football game with me in Anaheim, California. It was in Glover Stadium, the home field of Anaheim High School. The stands hold about eight thousand people and are packed every time the school plays.

Along about the third quarter, someone in the stands started to blow a whistle every time a play began. We had an injured player on the field and there was a time-out. I just happened to look up in the stands and purely by accident saw a kid in a blue jacket stand up, blow a whistle and then stick it in his pocket and sit down. There was a police officer over at the end of the bench and I walked over to him and said to him as I pointed, "Do you see that kid up there in the blue jacket next to the lady in the red coat?"

He said he did, and I told him, "He's got a whistle and he's blowing it and it's causing a lot of problems down here. So, will you go up there and get the whistle and tell him you'll give it back to him at the end of the game. Wave it to me when you have it and stick it into your pocket and we'll go on with the game."

The officer went up into the stands, stopped by the lady in the red coat, leaned over to the kid in the blue jacket, stuck his hand out and told the kid to give him the whistle. The kid gave him the whistle, the cop waved to me, put the whistle in his pocket and I turned around to the players and said, "All right, let's go on with the game."

Rosey was standing right behind me and shook his head in disbelief. "You mean to tell me that out of eight thousand people you could spot that one kid that's blowing a whistle and send a cop up there to get it from him?"

"Rosey, some guys' eyes are sharper than others. That's why you're the umpire and I'm the referee."

My son, Joel, taught me a lesson about my own whistle, which started me taking two to every game. He was playing with it and blew a piece of hard Christmas candy into it. I started a game between USC and Washington in the late fifties without a sound.

The films showed it. The fans knew it. They played the instant replay five times so no one could miss it. The coach who was covered with victory champagne knew it, but he accepted all the winning handshakes and hugs.

Letters were written by the losing team's supporters to the papers, to the league, to the world at large, and there was hardly anyone who could deny it. AN INADVERTENT WHISTLE HAD GIVEN THE TEAM THE GAME AND THE PLAY-OFFS.

A whistle was blown about .01 of a second too soon and the play was stopped before the defense could legally recover the fumble. Tough!!! The same rule book that says a touchdown is worth six points, says when a whistle blows while a ball is loose, it goes back to the team that fumbled it.

Constantly, coaches plead with officials to protect their quarterback. If four linemen had tackled that quarterback and he had been taken out of the game, hurt and unable to play again, it would have been a late whistle instead of a quick one. Maybe the whistle was blown quickly, or inadvertently because the official had his angle of vision blocked. The official could not see when the ball was ripped, squeezed away, or dropped by the quarterback.

John Madden, the Oakland Raiders coach, would always say to me before the game, "Hey, John. Protect my quarterback, will you?"

I'd tell him, "Well, I am not going to block for him. But don't worry, coach. I know all about quarterbacks because my son is one. I am not going to take my eyes off him."

Then, in the middle of the first quarter, his quarterback would throw the ball so late that the defensive linemen couldn't stop themselves from hitting him after he had released the ball.

Then Coach Madden would yell from the sidelines, "Hey, what about my quarterback? . . . . What about your son?"

"Well, tell him to throw the ball sooner." To this day, every time I see Coach Madden, he reminds me of those times.

It seems that about the middle of each season some quarterback is injured and a team's chances are ruined. When this happens we get an outcry from owners, coaches and the sports media saying, "Protect the quarterback," and "Why aren't quarterbacks afforded the same protection as kickers?"

Well, there are a few very important differences between a quarterback and a kicker. The kicker only has his protection when he keeps his identity as a kicker. If he gets the snap from the center and goes right into his kick, he is protected until he becomes a potential tackler, a time at which he may be legally blocked. If he gets a bad snap and starts to run he becomes a running back and may be tackled. He only regains his protection if he completely re-establishes himself as a kicker. If he kicks while he is running and gets knocked down, there is no foul, unless in the opinion of the referee he has been unnecessarily roughed.

A quarterback is *always* a potential runner, and when he starts to scramble he may be tackled the same as any other runner. If he suddenly stops and throws, or throws while he is running, he can be tackled like any other man who had possession of the ball. If he throws the ball while he is running, in time for the defense to avoid hitting him—and they belt him anyway—then they will be called for unnecessary roughness. It's difficult to expect the defense to keep from hitting him after they've been chasing him all over the field. The official decides if they should have been able to stop.

I don't think I've ever called a player for a late hit on a scrambling quarterback or kicker that I didn't get growls out of the defense, telling me that they lost their protection when they started to run. One time after I made a roughness call the owner of the team that fouled was so upset that he complained to the supervisor of officials. A week later, his own quarterback scrambled out of the pocket and was hit by two big defensive linemen just at the split second the ball left his hand. The quarterback was hurt on the play and missed the next four games of the season. The owner was then quoted as saying that something had to be done to protect the quarterbacks. Perhaps he should have talked to his own defensive coach about going after scrambling quarterbacks.

Whenever I hear about a quarterback being hurt I always want to know what he was doing when he got hit. Was he scrambling or did he hold the ball so long that he released it just as the defensive players were about to hit him? When I was Supervisor of Officials for the World Football League we had three quarterbacks hurt on the same weekend. The cry went up immediately that the officials weren't protecting them. I checked out each one, and in every case the quarterback was running with the ball, was tackled, and never did throw the ball. They were running backs at the time, and prone to all of the risks every other running back takes.

Maybe we could change the rules, to require all quarterbacks to wear polka dot uniforms so that everyone could identify them quickly, the officials could declare the ball dead as soon as anyone on the defense merely touched them. If anyone tackled them it would be a foul. We could make them promise that they will stay in the pocket and pass, and that we will blow the whistle the instant they start to scramble. Maybe we shouldn't allow them to run the ball past the line of scrimmage. These ideas would take most of the thrill out of the game, but they would help protect the physical health of the quarterback.

I am still waiting for the owner or coach, whose team was "hurt" by a quick whistle, to come forward and say, "I find no fault with the official. He protected my opponent's quarterback on that play and there will be a play sometime this season when he'll do the same thing for my quarterback. I'd rather have a healthy quarterback than a recovered fumble, any day."

Joe Namath probably said it better than anybody else, when he pointed out that if the defensive linemen and the linebackers do their job right, they get their prize, "Me."

At the Denver Bronco stadium, after the Big Orange crushes the enemy quarterback, they show a picture on their instant replay scoreboard of a horse opening up a sack and making room for the quarterback to fit in it. When the horse gets him in the sack he ties the rope to close it and smiles. The fans roar their approval. Besides coming to see their team win, one of the most important reasons to cheer is when the defensive rush puts the quarterback where he belongs—in the sack.

If the fans wrote to the league and said they didn't want to see the sack in the game because of the potential danger to the quarterback, and the owners complained in unison, and if the quarterbacks organized and boycotted games until they were guaranteed that football would be a non-collision sport, then you wouldn't have a coach yelling at a referee to protect his quarterback. And you certainly wouldn't have football edging closer to the first prosthetically thrown touchdown pass.

EIGHT

"What a catch!"
"God, what a catch!"
"Wow! What a play!"
"Did you see that?"

the crying voices
call out
before the stained-glass window of
television
on a tucked-in Sunday.

I don't know who has more control of the game—me or you. I run the game but you press the buttons that pay for the system that brings you professional football.

Sports television has trained the average fan's attention span to the length of time it takes to run an average play and show an average set of commercials. Television, with its spectacular play by play and instant replay dramatization, its full scale depiction of the personal pathos of athletes and their supporting cast, has made pro football what it is today. All so you can sit at home and with beer-sipping second-guessing, demand perfection from us, the field entertainers. You can shout and scream and call names confident that no one will challenge your opinion—unless, of course, your wife happens to be rooting for the other team.

MURPHY-78

Whatever the total effect of the athletic-television complex is on the world, it can make a hero or popular antihero out of a referee. I was always surprised when someone would recognize me while I was walking through an airport in a city where I had only been once or twice in my life. Many times people would come up to me and say, "Are you somebody?" or "Do I know you?" or "Should I be asking you for your autograph?"

One day I found out why people knew my face so well. We were on a plane with a television crew and the director told me, "The players have those big masks on and you can't see their faces, except when they're sitting on the bench with their helmets off. But you guys are just wearing those funny white hats, so we zero in on you a lot. And, especially you,"

101

he pointed to me. "You're so ugly, you just look like a referee." Every game is telecast somewhere in the country—either over the entire network, a certain segment of the country, or just back to the home city of the visiting team. I began to think I was some kind of celebrity. Fortunately, there's always someone who will let you know that you still put your shoes on one foot at a time.

I was at Shea Stadium one Sunday afternoon, working a game between the Minnesota Vikings and New York Jets. After the game I came out of the stadium and two kids came up to me. One of them said to me, "Hey, sign my book! Sign my autograph book!"

"O. K. son," and I signed, John McDonough—referee #11, National Football League. "There you go." His friend looked over and said, "Who is it?"

"The referee."

"The referee!!!" He took the book from him and tore out the page, wadded it up and threw it on the ground. Then he grabbed his friend's arm and said, "Come on. Let's go get some good ones."

"Come here, son," I said before they got away. The kid came back very slowly and there was a tear starting down his face.

"Here," I gave him a dollar.

"What's that for?"

"You just gave me a great story. I make a lot of speeches and what you just did when you tore up that piece of paper will make a good gag."

"Gee, thanks." He started to run off, then all of a sudden stopped short and came back once more. "Hey, mister. Sign it again, will you?"

Television has given me some interesting moments. I was working a game in San Diego a few years ago on a Saturday night. It was between the Chargers and the Rams. In the third quarter the Rams had the Chargers backed up to their own ten yard line, and it was San Diego's ball, first and ten. On the first play they had an ineligible receiver downfield and our umpire, Pat Harder, flagged him down. The Rams captains, Deacon Jones and Merlin Olsen, had the option of taking the penalty, making it first and fifteen, or refusing it, thereby making it second and ten. After a short conference they decided to refuse the penalty. We had developed a signal to indicate an ineligible receiver downfield in the early days of the American Football League. First, the referee would push his hands away from his chest which is the signal for pass interference. He would immediately follow this by patting his head with his right hand which is the signal for time-out on the referee. Well, all of this caused confusion because nobody understood the signal. We used it for about a year but when the National Football League developed a signal of both hands on top of the head, we junked our old signal and adopted theirs.

After Jones and Olsen refused the penalty, I guess I got a mental block, because I ran right out there in front of God and everybody, pushed my hands away from my chest, patted the top of my head with my right hand, and pointed to the Chargers. Then I crisscrossed my arms in front of me to indicate that the Rams had refused the penalty. The second I did it, I knew I'd blown it, but there was nothing I could do. The public address announcer was very magnanimous. He didn't say anything, but the thought flashed through my mind, "I wonder what Gil Stratton is saying on TV." So, Sunday I'm back home in Santa Ana, which is in the Los Angeles TV area, and Beth and I are watching the taped replay of the game. All of a sudden the play comes up and I tell her, "Well, here it comes, let's see what Gil says." He said, "The Ram captains are having a tough time trying to decide whether they want to take or refuse this penalty, but referee John McDonough will give the signal in a moment."

And then I run out and do that goofy routine, and show that the Rams refuse it. Gil didn't say anything for about five seconds, then finally he said, "Well, whatever that was, the Rams refused it."

Now, how is the Greatest Show on Earth handled for television. First let's talk about the money.

In 1977, a one minute commercial during a regular game cost $75,000. When I did Super Bowl IV in 1970 it was $150,000 for one minute. By the 1977 Superbowl it was $250,000 per commercial minute. How many commercial minutes do they have? They get seven each half of the game, three each quarter and one at the two minute warning.

In the early days of TV the fans in the stadium used to groan and shout, "Let's go, get on with the game, the hell with TV" but, you don't hear that anymore. I think they realize that this fourteen minutes is the price they pay for having great football brought into their homes when their team is on the road and the local stadium is empty.

Here's how it works. There's a fellow standing on the sidelines called the floor director. He is in communication with the TV director who is in the TV truck outside the stadium. In the control truck is a monitor picture for each of the five cameras in the stadium. Every one of these cameras is on all the time. They don't use film, they're just using up electricity. The director can push a button and send any one or any combination of them into your home.

The director tells the guy on the sidelines to tell the referee when they want a commercial. The floor director is very important to me because he's my only link with television. In the early days he would move up and down the sidelines following the ball, but would often get lost in the crowd of players, coaches, and photographers. Then they put a red hat on him, and he became known as the red hat man, a name that still is used by some TV directors today. But, the red hat didn't work either. Finally some of us referees suggested to the league office that he stay, during the whole game, on one of the thirty yard lines. They tried it and that is where he stands today.

The floor director uses only two signals. He folds his arms across his chest, and he holds his right hand over his heart. That's all he has to do. The referee out on the field is the only one who pays any attention to him. When the director tells him to signal for a commercial, he stands at the thirty yard line and folds his arms across his chest, which means the TV people want the air at the next normal opportunity. When I see his signal I point to the ground and nod my head. That means to tell the director in the truck, "The referee knows we want it."

You never cut away for a commercial during an offensive drive. The normal opportunity is usually after a kick, a recovered fumble by the defense, and intercepted pass, a score of any kind, an injured player, or a team time-out. The referee will step into the clear, and, (1) crisscross his arms over his head, (2) point towards both goal lines simultaneously with his arms outstretched, and (3) tap himself on his head with his right hand. This means, it's time-out, it's for television, and charge it to me. At this time you will usually hear the public address announcer say, "There's time out on the field." The TV play-by-play announcer will then say a cue phrase, something like, "The broadcast of the National Football League will continue in one minute after this message."

The TV director out in the truck starts the commercial tape and while it's on, the floor director stands with his right hand over his heart which tells me the commercial is on the air. Fifty seconds after the start of the commercial he'll drop his hand to his side and I'll declare the ball ready for play, which means the offense has thirty seconds to get the ball snapped. So if it all works out right, the offensive team is just coming out of the huddle when the television returns you to the stadium.

I think almost every pro and college football official will agree that the instant replay is one of the best things that ever happened because it will show us right over ninety percent of the time.

Most officials also think instant replay helps fans appreciate the game on television. They don't, however, appreciate being maligned by commentators who don't know the rules or understand the mechanics well enough to know whether an official has or has not made a mistake.

Every year it is suggested that we use TV replays to check the officials' calls. It would take at least twenty cameras to cover every side-line, goal line and end line, along with each combination of players in various positions.

It has been estimated that it would take between sixty to ninety seconds to read and make a decision on each instant replay. Would you like to spend ten, fifteen or even twenty dollars to see a game and have to wait a minute to a minute and a half every four or five plays while someone reviewed the instant replay tape?

The NFL office estimates that it would cost close to fifty million dollars a year to have enough fully trained cameramen and equipment to put a mechanical eye on every angle of the playing field. If there were five hundred protested or missed calls every fifty thousand plays (a one percent error factor) it would cost *one hundred thousand* dollars for each one.

When people talk about using millions of dollars of electronic gadgetry to double check the officials and slow up and game for the fans in the stadium, it might be well to stop and consider this.

In the 1977 season the NFL played 84 preseason games, 196 regular season games, 6 playoff games, one Super Bowl, and one Pro Bowl, for a total of 288 games. They averaged just over 160 plays per game.

Taking 288 games times 160 plays equals 46,080 plays for the season. A one percent error factor would allow for 460.8 mistakes. However, they usually have five or six *really* controversial plays per season. But, let's say they have ten. If they blow ten plays per season they have an error factor of 0.000217%, which is 217 ten thousandths of one percent. I have never heard of any business that delivers that kind of accuracy, including the electronic gadgets that are supposed to be perfect.

One thing the TV cameras cannot do is give you depth perception. Only the human eye can do this instantaneously. The camera can give width and height but no depth. Very often it is the dimension of depth that governs the official's call. Later, a film with a view from the side shows the official was right all along.

Something else to consider in regard to using this kind of machinery is what would keep the players' association from filing an injunction on a game and making the league take that play or a series of plays to a court for arbitration in making a final decision on a call? And don't tell me there can be observers from each team up in the booth evaluating each play—no way.

Although I like the idea of instant replay as part of television packaging of football, I have to agree with my friend, Curt Gowdy, one of the foremost TV game announcers. At the 1976 Rose Bowl Kickoff Luncheon in Pasadena, California, Curt was master of ceremonies and made this statement:

> *I don't know about the rest of you but I am getting kind of tired of people talking about using the replay to check up on the work of the officials. I've probably seen as many games as any man alive and I can count on one hand the times when I saw a play I actually thought was called wrongly. A play that may have altered the outcome of a game. Yet here we are talking about using some electronic gadgets for those few plays. I think it's terribly unnecessary and ridiculous. I think it's time we forgot about this stuff and let our fine officials do their job and get on with the game and enjoy it.*

He got a tremendous ovation from the four thousand fans on hand.

Up until the time that I retired from Sunday officiating for the NFL I didn't have much of a chance to watch a game on television unless it was my day off or a Monday night when I wasn't working. When I started watching games on the air more frequently, both in the NFL and to check my officials' work in the World Football League I was appalled at how many errors some of the expert commentators, and other TV announcers were making.

During one game, the announcer said to the expert commentator, who happened to be a former player, "This is the fourth time in two weeks we've had a defensive holding foul on a pass play. Why isn't that pass interference?"

The former player said, "The way that is, if the holding is in the direction of the pass it's ruled as a pass interference, and if it's away from the direction of the pass, it's defensive holding."

"Oh, no!" I yelled. "There he goes. He's just made another new rule."

"Maybe he hasn't, John. Maybe you've just had too much football," Beth suggested.

"No, he's wrong. What the rule book says, is, 'If holding is before the ball is in the air, it's defensive holding, and if the holding is after the ball is in the air it's pass interference.'" The expert commentator had misinformed millions of people.

The next week, right before the game I was refereeing, I got the two head coaches together to clarify the difference between pass interference and holding on a pass play. Sure enough, one of them had been watching that game on TV and started to argue that I was wrong.

One of the most common errors of announcers and instant replay analysts is what they say about flags thrown on a running play. An announcer will say, "Well, that call was a little late."

First of all, if you have a clipping call—what we call a spot foul—the official has to come in close enough to get his flag on the place where the foul occurred, because that is one of the spots from where the penalty might be marked off. He usually has to work his way around the players in order to get there, and this takes a little time. Sometimes the clip occurs after the play has been called dead. The man with the ball has been tackled and someone clips another player. When this call is flagged the announcer and the public may think it is late because everyone has seen the ball declared dead.

"Why do you get so picky? The play is over, what's the difference?" Well, the difference is that some poor ball player—who thought the play was over—may be on his way to the hospital with his knee going in the wrong direction. The foul *must* be called because the rules' makers don't want anyone taking any "free shots." You can't allow players to take cheap hits at each other, hits that have nothing to do with a legitimate defensive or offensive effort or maneuver.

Commentators, through no fault of their own, at times won't be following the most important element of the play—or at least the one that is going to become important—the foul. The cameras will come in and follow the wrong players down the field, while over on the other side a man is being fouled. The TV doesn't show that and then the announcers wonder why pass interference was called when they were looking at two people who were legitimately fighting for the ball.

It really bothers me when slow motion replays are used in an irresponsible manner. Slow it down, even with stop action and people believe this is how the game is played, that this is how the officials see it. The game is played at normal speed, not in slow motion. They will show it in slow motion and say look at him holding, when if you see it at normal speed the guy barely brushed his arm as he went by him. And that's not a holding infraction.

I saw a fumble on the ground and a man reached out to scoop it in and there was a pileup. When everyone was untangled the other team had the ball. Now, if an official got in there as close as the zoom lens puts you to see how the ball went back and forth between the players, he'd be on his way to his own funeral the next day. The zoom lens gets in there and they stop it on one split second and an announcer will say, "You see this man has the ball," when he never legally has possession.

Another misunderstanding that occurs from time to time is when a player from each team simultaneously gains possession of a fumble. By rule, the ball is always awarded to the team that last had possession.

Now on a pass play, if two players—on opposing teams—go up for a pass and they come down with it, it is what we call a simultaneous catch and interception. They both have control, they both have possession, but the ball belongs to the offense. If it's in the end zone it is a touchdown.

What would you say about a play where *no one* has possession of the ball? It is just lying there, ten yards away from the closest player. What would you expect the officials to do, and how would you describe it if you were a TV announcer? You're the referee or the TV announcer, go ahead, what would you say?

Far be it from me to downgrade any former coaches or players who are now TV analysts. By and large they do an excellent job of telling the public about the plays, strategy, and techniques of playing the game. However, when they start to talk about rules and the work of the officials, they sometimes become "Directors of Sports Misinformation." Here are a few examples that I personally have heard.

ANNOUNCER: "He called him for offensive pass interference before the quarterback threw the ball."

EXPERT (FORMER PRO COACH): "The referee (it was the field judge) must have thought the ball had been thrown."

CORRECT RULING: Pass interference by the offense is prohibited from the time the center snaps the ball until the pass is touched because the offense knows it is to be a pass. The restriction on the defense starts when the ball is thrown and ends when it is touched.

SITUATION: A punt hit a receiver on the leg at the six yard line. One of the kickers picked it up and ran into the end zone. The ball was brought back and awarded to the kickers, first and goal, on the six.

ANNOUNCER: "The ball hit him on the leg. Doesn't that make it anybody's ball?"

EXPERT (FORMER ALL-PRO PLAYER): "Yes, but the ref (it was the back judge) blew the whistle so it comes back to where it was when he blew it."

CORRECT RULING: The kicking team cannot advance their own kick once it crosses the line. It remains a kick until it is possessed. When the receivers merely touch the kick, it makes it a "hot potato" and either team may recover it. The receivers may advance it, but if the kickers recover it it is dead and their ball at that point.

SITUATION: Two safety men. One signaled for a fair catch but the other man caught the punt and ran. The official killed the play. Then he gave the receivers first and ten at the spot where the second safety man, who *did not* signal, caught the ball.

ANNOUNCER: "He didn't signal for a fair catch, why can't he run?"

EXPERT (FORMER PLAYER): "The ref (it was the field judge) must have thought he was the one who signalled."

CORRECT RULING: The official was correct. When one man signals for a fair catch, what he is saying, is, "I give up the right for all players on my team to advance the ball in return for protection for me personally if I catch the kick."

ANNOUNCER: "What's the difference between a muff and a fumble?"

EXPERT (FORMER ALL-PRO QUARTERBACK): "It is a technical thing. I think it has something to do with a pass."

CORRECT RULING: You can only fumble a ball if you have clear possession. If a loose ball (kick, pass, or fumble) bounces off the hands or body in an unsuccessful attempt to gain possession, it is a muff. Note: Every time a receiver bobbles a kick and the announcer says, "He fumbled it," over 100,000 officials, from Pop Warner to pro, groan.

SITUATION: Illegal contact occurred and the field judge threw his flag, went to the spot and with his back toward the referee, gave the Pass Interference signal and pointed to the defense.

ANNOUNCER (FORMER ALL-PRO PLAYER): "That is the worst thing I have ever seen. He called Pass Interference on the offense, then realized that they were the home team and changed his call to the defense." Later in the game he referred to this play several times, calling it the turning point in the game.

CORRECT RULING: When Pass Interference is called there is a key in the mechanics of the official making the call that will tell any knowledgeable person immediately if the call is on the offense or the defense.

If the official making the interference call stays at the spot of the interference it is always on the defense. He will wait there for the referee to come to him because that is where you will award the passers the ball.

If the official throws his flag and runs back to the line of scrimmage to the referee it is always on the offense, because the penalty will be marked off from the previous spot.

During the 1977 football season, one prominent TV announcer spent three or four minutes and a couple of replays explaining that the officials had erred because they did not follow the rule about "Intercepting Momentum" on a kicking play.

That night I heard three local sportscasters talk about the same subject and the following morning a sportswriter covered it in his column. It must have been absolutely ludicrous to every football official in the country. Why? Because the play was a punt, fielded on the one yard line. Intercepting Momentum has to do with pass plays, not kicks. When was the last time you heard about anyone intercepting a kick? They intercept passes, not kicks.

The ideal answer, of course, would be for football telecasting to become more instructive. Maybe a former NFL official could be placed on a television crew to add some light banter and expertise to the show.

Pardon me. I have to go into the next room and turn on the TV set. They might come up with some new and strange rulings, and I'd hate to miss them.

NINE

You just can't trust those refs. They took a touchdown away from us and then they missed calling a fumble near the goal line and our guy scored on the next play. We're completely at their mercy. You just can't trust them.

Myrna Feld
Denver Super Bowl Lady
January, 1978

Some people just can't fathom that anyone can be impartial and unemotional about a football game, *especially* the officials. They can't see how we can be involved in the game and not be aware of the point spread or that every foul called could possibly determine the outcome of the game, the championship and the world. An official, even at the lowest level of competition, sure as hell isn't going to do anything as inimical as trying to influence the outcome of any game.

I don't know where people get the idea, but the notion seems to exist that officials balance out fouls during a game. That possibly before each game, or after each play, we make decisions as to what calls we'll make to keep the game even, or, if it serves the purpose, one-sided. I wouldn't be sur-

prised if thoughts were conjured up that pictured us sitting around trying to figure out the best way to keep the home town fans happy. I am sure there must be someone who feels we have favorite teams and that we go out there to help them in any way that we can. That maybe we have a pool we bet in, and then go out on the field and try our best to win all of the money in the pot. It must be easy for fans who want to believe that we go out there to balance out the fouls called, or show our partiality for one team by throwing our flags in the direction of the other. Announcers, sportswriters, fans and even coaches show a lack of knowledge of how officials operate when they say, "The refs are evening things up out there."

We don't even things up. When someone says that an official is "evening things," they are accusing him of being dishonest. And one thing that has been consistent with every official I have come into contact with for thirty-five years is that they have an extremely high sense of integrity. I think that is one of the reasons they become officials.

The official who would try to even things up by calling a foul on one team after he has called one on the other would find himself in real trouble. It would come out looking so ridiculous and obvious that he soon would be out of a job. For certain, other officials would refuse to work with him.

The only people I have ever known who tried to "even up" were officials of junior athletic teams. When they worked high school games they thought it would best serve the interest of the game by trying to make things *even*. When we got them into a recognized organization we either cured them or dropped them.

Officials, as a general rule, are not at all interested in the publicity given to a game. They are aware of what is riding on it, whether it is a championship game, or a rivalry. Officials react to these kinds of situations by being on top of absolutely every play. Games played by the best teams, in many respects, are the easiest to work because the teams are evenly matched; the players commit less fouls. The team units are more cohesive and consequently the players make fewer mistakes.

If I flew to Boston to work a game between the Patriots and the Redskins, I would have never read the Boston or Washington papers on the day of the game or the week before, and I wouldn't have listened to the radio or television about that week's game. And, officials do not allow a coach or member of his staff to point out things about their opponent. We would not allow them to, as the saying goes, "set us up."

Officials who reach the level of the NFL have an enormous sense of fairness, that has been honed, refined and fire-hardened by hundreds, and perhaps thousands of games in high school, college and university ball. Officials aren't out there to zero in on any particular player. I have never been told by any supervisor of officials to watch anyone specifically. One play at a time. One game at a time, is how you work. Often when a foul is called on a player, the fans, coaches and writers are sure their verbal warnings have finally made us, the officials, watch him. Not true.

If a player has a flag thrown on him it is because on *that single play* he committed a foul, and one or more of the officials spotted it and called it. If the game film later show that he committed a previous foul and it wasn't called, it is simply because none of the officials were looking at him at that split second and it was missed. I have had players come up to me and say, "Did you see him hold me?"

The answer is obvious, "No, if I had seen him I would have called it."

In one pro game I officiated in the mid sixties one of the teams did not commit any fouls. It was so intriguing to our supervisor, Mel Hein, that he looked at our game film five times. He said there was one foul—the team didn't have enough guys on the line of scrimmage for one play. A player had lined up a foot too far into the backfield instead of on the line. It just so happened that this game was so one-sided that no one got intense enough to make mistakes and foul. Generally if two teams are relatively equal the fouls will be about the same. Fans should not be misled by the statistics of penalties as they appear in the press.

When you look in the paper and see that one team was penalized, let's say one hundred yards, and the other team was penalized about thirty yards, the first thing someone might say is, "The officials were really leaning on that team."

Well, there could have been just as many fouls called against one team as the other. The penalty yardage a team *refuses* to take is not recorded, so on the surface you can get a misconception of what really happened. If all the statistics were recorded you would know the number of fouls that were called in the game and the total amount of yardage that *could* have been marched off against each team. If these facts were printed the game would probably not appear so unbalanced. For example,

	No. of Fouls	Refused	Yards Penalized
Hawks	12	0	95
Wolves	10	4	30

So the Wolves refused four fouls and the yardage looks out of balance but there were only two more fouls called on the Hawks.

Another thing that will make the yardage look one-sided is a pass interference call on the defense. If a team commits defensive pass interference on a thirty-five yard pass they are awarded the ball at the spot of the interference and thirty-five yards is added to the "yards penalized total."

Another thing you'll hear someone say when there seems to be an uneven number of fouls and when the score is one-sided, is, "Well, the team won but they committed a lot of fouls."

The chances are that in a one-sided game the winning team was on offense a lot, and there are more ways of fouling on offense than there are on defense. Defensive guys are allowed to use their hands to push, pull and fight their way in there. Offensive guys are prohibited from using their hands so that too affects the balance. To say that officials were out to get one team—even though they may have won—is certainly not a fair statement.

I've become a great fan of James Michener. I think I have read everything he's written. His book, *Sports in America,* is one of the finest treatments of sports ever written; however I've got to take exception with one point he makes. He quotes Leonard Koppett's theory on the home team advantage. Koppett's conclusions infer that after a while, fans start "getting to" the officials and the officials respond by calling fouls against the other team, making it almost inevitable that the home team will win. I don't agree that the home crowd "gets to" the officials and causes them to favor the locals. What happens is that the home rooters get on the visiting team, causing them to get desperate and lose their poise and start to foul. And when they foul the officials are going to make them pay for it. I have found that with the tougher, more disciplined teams, the teams that have played together long and well as a unit, it doesn't matter where they are playing. The tougher the crowd gets on them the more they are able to dig in and not allow anything to get to them. They "keep their cool."

An unpoised visiting team will allow the fans to get to them and respond by taking chances they normally wouldn't take. They might take some dangerous risks, miss their blocks and reach out and hold other players late in the game, when they're tired and frustrated. Then the yellow flags fly and everyone says the crowd got to the officials and they started calling them on the visitors. What really happened was that the visitors started to foul more. That's all.

A high school game might be between two schools that are only a few miles apart, so the crowds are about equal in partisanship for each team. You go to a Stanford-Cal or a USC-UCLA game and half the stadium is for one team and half for the other. Only in the big intersectional rivalries is the crowd going only one way.

When the Los Angeles Rams go back East to play the New York Giants, they're lucky if they've got twenty people rooting for them. The Giant fans are going to holler and yell and call names.

Fans get irate, and say officials had a field day. That they had those flags out and were throwing them all over the place. That we ruined the game, and really stunk up the place. We took sport's justice and set it back at least a hundred years. Well, officials would love to go through every game and not have to call one foul. To send our cards into the league office without one penalty listed on them would be cause for a big celebration.

Coaches can get caught in an emotional trap when they review game films and come up with such a winning statement as, "That call cost us the ball game."

They have the idea that the official actually knew that the call was going to cost them the game. Maybe the call did cost them the ball game, but it wasn't the official who cost them anything. Go find number 68 or number 57 who held on the play that was called back with penalty yardage. That's the cause for the losing game, not the call. The official sees the foul and throws the flag. He isn't aware, nor does he care, if the call he makes is going to be to one team's advantage or not. He has no way of knowing when he throws the flag what may happen in the next split second of play. The team that fouled may throw a pass on the play and the pass may be intercepted and may be run back for a touchdown. Obviously in that case, the scoring team will refuse the penalty and take the touchdown. Now how is an official supposed to know that?

Officials have often been accused of being responsible for an injury, too. People get the idea that if they had called the foul, the gross clip or hold or bad pop wouldn't have happened. The conclusion is that since an official didn't make the call on a play when a player got hurt, that the injury was partly or entirely due to the official. The official had nothing to do with anyone getting hurt. The player who committed the foul is the one who is responsible.

I'll grant you that every official on the field wishes he could have the play over again. He hates to think that a kid got hurt by a foul play and the guy got away with it. That he actually got a cheap shot in and didn't get caught in the act. But it happens and it's going to continue to happen. You can't get them all. There are seven guys out there watching twenty-two players so you're not going to get them all, but somehow people get the idea that if the official had called the foul that kid wouldn't be in the hospital. He's still going to be in the hospital. Calling the foul wouldn't have prevented the injury.

I had a situation one time where the quarterback was running with the football and got hurt. As I said earlier, when he's running, he doesn't have any more protection than any other runner. He's just as vulnerable to the guys who weigh out at 265 as a regular running back. Once he throws the ball he has protection. If he doesn't go out and try and block somebody after he throws the ball then he has protection because he is still the passer. But until he throws it he's a runner. Now, here comes a quarterback and he's late. He throws the ball but he's used up so much of his time back there trying to find an open receiver that the player or players chasing him can't avoid hitting him. The call becomes a judgment one for the referee. Was there roughing the passer?

In this particular situation the quarterback was running and it looked like he was going to go forward, past the line of scrimmage and try to run for a gain, then at the last second he found a receiver and fired the ball. Just as he released the ball the defensive player was right up into his chest and crushed him. The lineman's head went right up underneath the quarterback's chin and broke his jaw. (I read later he swallowed two teeth.) No foul called, because I had determined that he had released the ball too late. There were claims by the quarterback's team that the defensive player hit him with the cast he was wearing on his arm, but that wasn't true, it was the top of his head gear that got him. The quarterback was through for the season with his jaw wired shut. The league office backed us up on it. Everyone who saw the films could see that the call was right.

Some of the writers in discussing the incident would lead you to believe that if a foul had been called the player wouldn't have been hurt. If there had been a foul and I had called it, the quarterback still would have gone to the hospital. I felt sorry for the player, but the longer the quarterback keeps the ball the greater his jeopardy.

The rule is that when a man is obviously out of the play he can't be tackled or hit. When he's got the ball he's open game. Good linebackers tell you, "My job is to go in there and find the guy with the seed, sort him out and crunch him." With a job description like that, somebody's bound to go to the hospital once in a while.

Some coaches will run up to an official after the second quarter and yell, shaking their fists and swinging their programs and game plans. Sometimes they do it for the crowd but I think more often it's just to let off game pressure.

It's the first chance they have to "get on" you without picking up a fifteen yard penalty. And, as long as they're not violent, or talk to us in an abusive manner, we'll go right along with them. One of the occupational hazards of being an official is being a part-time whipping boy for the coaches.

Weeb Eubank, the New York Jets coach, chased me right up to the locker room door once. He wasn't happy either. It was at halftime in a game between the Jets and San Diego Chargers.

That day, October 13, 1963, in San Diego Weeb had good reason to be concerned. Just before the end of the half, New York attempted a thirty-five yard field goal and the wind carried the ball around the goalposts. It never crossed over the crossbars between the uprights. Weeb thought the ball had gone between the posts. Had I been standing next to him on the sidelines, I'm sure I would have agreed with him. He was irate and blamed me for missing the call because I made it from so far back. At that time, with only five officials, the referee ruled on the success or failure of a field goal, standing behind the kicker.

"Why don't you put two guys down there right under the goal posts and let them look straight up. That way there won't be any kind of guessing about the call. Why are you trying to call it from way back there?" Weeb asked.

"I think you've got a point, Weeb. Tell you what you do. You write to Thurlo McCrady, our supervisor, with the suggestion. I'll put it in my report and ask if my crew can try it in a game. If it works out we might be able to change the mechanics all over the league."

He wrote the letter and I put it in my report and the following Wednesday I got a call from Thurlo McCrady telling me to work out the mechanics with my crew and try out Weeb's suggestion. We tried it for three weeks and it worked well.

The referee is no longer responsible for looking to see if the ball goes between the uprights. It's now up to the field judge and the back judge, who are standing under the posts with their eyes focused upwards. This system is now the mechanics in all of pro ball, college ball, and many high school leagues. The referee is back to his primary duty of being sure there is no roughing of the kicker or the holder or any illegal blocks to protect them.

The colleges widened the posts to encourage field goal kicking and to improve scoring possibilities. This also started with the coaches. They asked that the goal posts be moved up to the goal line instead of being on the end line, at the back of the end zone.

The NCAA rules committee thought that would create an extra danger so they decided to leave them on the end line but spread the space between the uprights. This widened the area of aim for the place kicker, thus giving him and the offense one more advantage.

A few years later, the pros wanted to discourage the use of the field goal. They changed the kicking rule so that if you missed on an attempted field goal, the other team would get the ball, first and ten, back at the original line of scrimmage—the "previous spot" as football people call it. At the same time they moved their goal posts back to the end line.

Every year the competition committee of the National

Football League considers possible rule changes in a continuing effort to create a balance between offensive and defensive play. They are also interested in any rules that will improve the safety of the game and increase the entertainment value for the fan.

One of my objections to the present overtime rule is that the first team that scores, wins. Their opponents aren't guaranteed a chance to have the ball. I think the rule should be changed so that the first team that scores wins, providing both teams have had at least one offensive opportunity.

For example, the Dolphins are playing the Cardinals and the score is tied at the end of regulation play. The Dolphins win the overtime coin toss and elect to receive. They catch the kick, run it back to the Cardinal twenty-five, kick a field goal and the game is over, under the present rules.

I would like to see the NFL use the same rule we had in the WFL. After the Dolphins scored they would have to kick off to the Cardinals. The Cardinals would now have a chance to score. If they failed to score and the Dolphins regained the ball, in any way, the game would be over. If the Cardinals scored a field goal, the score would again be tied and they would play until one team scored. If the Cardinals scored a touchdown, they would be the winners. If, at the start of the overtime, the Dolphins did not score and kicked to the Cardinals, the rule would be just as it is now, the first team to make any kind of a score would be the winner.

No matter what the final score is, no matter how many "ifs," every overtime period always starts with the possibility of being the longest game ever played.

One of the greatest official's signals anyone ever created came up in a high school game with a crew, headed by my good friend, Nick Vorona. He was the referee in a game between Mater Dei and St. Anthony High, in Eddie West Field, Santa Ana, California's municipal stadium.

The umpire saw two players go off the line at the snap of the ball and become entangled in each other's arms. He threw his flag at them, but as they unlocked themselves he realized that the holder had the same color shirt on as the holdee—they were both on the same team. And, there is no foul for holding your own teammate.

The play was for a thirty-five yard gain and the umpire quickly ran down to tell Nick what had happened. Nick waved his hands above his head as if he were wiping something out of the sky and then ran to the spot where the flag was laying. He picked it up and ran to the fifty yard line, faced the press box, put the flag in his mouth, bit it, and then stuffed it back in the umpire's pocket. The reporters in the press box howled and asked me what kind of signal was that.

"I think you got the word didn't you? The guy didn't have a foul and he's gonna have to eat his flag." Most good officials will admit when they've made a miscall. I understand that the Canadian Football League has a signal for this type of mistake. The official will come out into the clear, put his flag on the ground, then wave his arms over the flag with the same signal he uses for an incompleted pass.

I think that would be a good idea for American football. Maybe there should even be a set of signals developed that coaches can make to officials whenever they are disappointed or angry over an official's call. It would save the voices of the coaches. The people in the stands, after they learned what the signals meant, would know what the coaches were "thinking."

TEN

I was playing for the Patriots in 1960 and got a knee injury. It felt like people were jabbing me with red hot pokers. When the doctor said, "Let's move him," I looked up at you and you looked right at me and said, "Take it easy, son. You're going to be o.k. You'll be back in here."

I felt there was one person out there looking out for me.

Lee Phelps, Santa Ana, California

Just because officials are precise, accurate and automatic in our work and don't smile, doesn't mean we lack feelings. I have felt damn sorry for players and coaches, and been touched deeply by tributes given to them by fans.

Keith Lincoln played for the San Diego Chargers for a number of years and then they traded him. After a few years, they traded back for him. I was refereeing the game when Lincoln came back. The stadium was decked out with banners painted

WELCOME BACK HONEST ABE,

and

SAN DIEGO IS LINCOLN COUNTRY.

He had only been back a few days so he was used mostly

on specialty teams, to return punts, kicks, and kickoffs, and maybe run one or two scrimmage plays. He was standing back by the goalpost ready to receive a kickoff and I said to him, "I guess it's nice to be home."

And he looked around the stadium and said, "How about that. Can you believe these people? Isn't it great of them to come out and give a guy an ovation like this?"

I said it sure was a nice tribute, and by then the television guy had taken his arm down and we were ready for the kickoff. I signalled for play to begin, Keith got the ball, and ran almost to midfield before he was driven out of bounds. As he was hit, one of his legs was caught and twisted by the tackle and pileup. We got everybody else up, but Keith. The doctors came then, and he was taken off the field on a stretcher. It was announced that Keith Lincoln had a broken leg and was out for the season. About a half hour later he was rolled out in a wheelchair with his leg in a cast. There was no way the game could go on. Even the opponents were cheering for the guy. He got a standing ovation and everyone in the stadium was in tears.

There was pathos again on November 12, 1972, when the 49ers were playing Baltimore in Candlestick Park. In this particular game the starting quarterback was shaken up on a play. I was standing there looking down at the young quarterback who was knocked about semi-cold. He was all right, but his bell was rung and he was going to have to sit out of the game for a while. I wondered what everyone was cheering about and then I looked over at the Baltimore side of the field and there was the gifted Johnny Unitas warming up to go in for the injured player. The San Francisco fans were letting him know that he was still one of the best there was, even though he was playing against them. But he got blitzed on the very first play. The reaction of the crowd was amazing. The minute he got sacked the place just went wild. It was his only play. He was injured.

When he didn't get up, the crowd went into a deep groan. He sat there on the turf as the team attendants administered to him, and the other quarterback came back into the game. Unitas limped off, his head down. Here was a guy, a veteran of all that football, who obviously was hurt more than just physically. As he left the field, they gave him another ovation. I couldn't help feeling a deep sense of sorrow for him. And I had a lot of respect for the 49er fans who gave such a fine round of applause for a guy who was playing against them.

In Super Bowl IV I saw Joe Kapp as quarterback for the Minnesota Vikings fight desperately against the Kansas City Chiefs. It was a losing battle all the way because the

Chiefs weren't about to drop that game. Joe was sacked late in the game and shaken up. As he sat there on the ground, I couldn't help feeling sorry for him. He was a lonely looking figure that day in New Orleans as he walked off the field. The sun was going down, he had given it everything he had to give. As he moved slowly to the bench you could feel the last of his energy had been spent.

Later I came to know Joe better and respect him as a person when I worked on two movies with him—*Semi-Tough* and *Two Minute Warning*.

I felt badly for a coach once—Lou Saban. Lou was coaching the Denver Broncos then. He strained for his guys all the time and whenever two or three penalties piled up against them he'd go crazy. I've always thought that if a coach wasn't out there rooting for his team then he wasn't a very good coach. I think Lou is one of the exceptionally good ones. It was the two-minute warning at the end of the game, and I went to him to ask him who his captains were. He said only one, his quarterback. I asked, "Only one, Lou?"

"Only one. I just want my quarterback to call time-out."

I said, "Okay." But if ever there was a time I wanted to give a coach some advice it was then. However, we're not out there for that.

Towards the very end of the game, within the last thirty seconds, the Denver quarterback went back to throw and when he couldn't find his receivers open, began running up the sidelines. He gained about thirty yards before he was tackled. There was a huge pile of players on top of him so he wasn't able to tell the officials "time-out." The other Denver players were jumping in front of the officials yelling for a time-out but all the officials could tell them was that time-out could only be called by their captain.

In the case of a choice of a penalty the referee may designate a player as captain if the captain is in some way not able to answer the choice of options. The official will then turn to the other player and say, "You're the captain, what do you want?" But, not in this case. I would be advising a player if I asked him if he wanted his team to call a time-out, thereby indicating to him that I thought it would be a good idea.

And so, in Denver, the clock ran down to double zeros. I felt sorry for Lou and the Broncos because if they had been able to get the clock stopped they would have had a chance for a field goal attempt. I am not criticizing Lou. I think at that time it was just an oversight. Later, the league office and the observer of officials at the game asked me about this situation. As I remember, Ronnie Gibbs was the observer, and we told him that we asked Lou specifically about this, and he said only one. And when Lou talked to the office later about this he said that he had given us "only one captain."

Fights aren't what pro football is selling, but they are still part of the ticket price. Television doesn't cover them. It focuses in on another part of the field, probably to keep the kids at home from seeing the violence that can come from a bunch of men whose basic aim is to knock each other down.

I hate to see a fight start in a football game. Some fans don't mind, I know, but for the officials, it's hell. I always tried to snuff them out before they started. If players were just pushing each other around I wasn't going to eliminate anyone from the ball game. But when words weren't enough and things got hot, I'd have to jump right in there between them.

One thing officials always try to remember when coming in to break up a fight is that you do not come up behind a player. You step in between those involved, from the front and make sure they know you're there. I developed the habit of jumping in between the fighters and pushing one back with my shoulder while shoving the other one away with my hands. I always amazed myself when I saw the films of the game the following week. There I was among guys three inches to a foot taller than me, fifty to seventy-five pounds heavier, with the only safety being my black and white striped shirt. Once a commissioner of a high school game came down onto the field to try to mediate along with the officials, and one of the assistant coaches, not knowing who he was, charged him and hit him for getting in the way of the "regulars" who were trying to restore order.

I worked one game that had a little extra action in it for Bobby Maples of the Oilers. Houston was trying him in different positions. It was a game between the Jets and the Oilers, on October 16, 1966, and one place he played was back, blocking for the kicker.

It was late in the game and Bobby had just blocked another player. Then I saw both of them on their knees facing each other. I didn't know what happened but Bobby was enraged. He hit the other guy so hard under the chin that he stood him straight up on his feet. Then Bobby came after him for a second shot.

I tried to step between them and he pushed me out of the way. "Knock it off," I hollered. "You're out of the game." He turned and gave me a startled look. I could see all over his face the thought, "Oh my God, I hit the referee." He ran quickly to the sidelines. I went over to his coach, Wally Lemm, pointed at Bobby, and said, "He's gone."

If a player hits a game official in anger he can be suspended for life. A shove in anger can also be interpreted as ground for suspension. In Bobby's case it was instant remorse, and I could tell there was no anger. It was simply a mistake. The game was over a few plays after the incident, and he came up to me and apologized. I told him I knew he didn't mean it. I also told him that Commissioner Joe Foss was in the press box and would want a report.

A New York writer was at the dressing room area after the game and he said the writers in the press box asked him to get my comments for them and the other members of the media. I told him that I wasn't allowed to talk to the press without permission from the commissioner. Just as I said that, Commissioner Joe Foss walked up.

"Go ahead John, I want to hear it, too." His concern was like everyone else's, "Did he hit you?" I told both of them that he didn't, that he just pushed me aside. The newspaper guy asked again, "He didn't hit you?" I said, "No sir. If he had hit me I wouldn't be here talking to you," and they both laughed.

The next day the incident was reported in the Houston Chronicle and the credit for my last remark was given to Johnny Fouch, our rookie back judge, who had left the stadium while I was being interviewed.

I cut the clipping out of the paper and sent it to Fouch with a note saying, "Here's your press notice, rookie. It's okay when you get credit for what I do, but when you steal my funny lines, I get a little irritated."

Later I told Joe that if I thought Bobby hit me on purpose I would want him suspended, but I was certain that he didn't know who I was. Joe acted on what I said, and Bobby's career continued.

In the early AFL days we'd sometimes get two games in the same city on consecutive Sundays. With only eight teams in the AFL it was bound to happen, so, Frank and Alma Kirkland, our field judge and his wife, and Beth and I took a week's vacation and visited New Orleans.

The next Sunday when I returned to Rice Stadium, Bobby Maples was outside the dressing room waiting for me. He thanked me for what I had told the commissioner. I asked him what happened and he said, "I was fined but the money wasn't the big thing. Did you ever get chewed out by a marine general?" Joe Foss was a general in the Air Defense Command.

"I don't think you'll ever have any trouble out of the Oilers either 'cause they all heard him chew me up."

That week Bobby Maples was made Houston's offensive center, and he did such a fantastic job that he became the center in the All-Star Game for the Eastern Team.

I was the referee for that game. It was played in a downpour at the new Oakland Coliseum, on a miserable day for everyone. We used many towels to keep the balls clean. The quarterbacks and the centers would also wipe their hands on my towel. Especially when the center had to snap for a kick. Once, late in the game, when the Eastern Team was going to kick, Bobby came over to use my towel and I kiddingly said to him, "What would you do without me," and he said, "If it wasn't for you I wouldn't even be here." You can't help but like a guy like Bobby Maples. It was a thrill to see him playing with the 1977 Denver Broncos.

Games have been stopped for impossible fan behavior, fighting, delays for television and the ritual of a triumphant gallop of horses onto the side of the field when a team scored, but I was working a game that stopped for the most beautiful reason of all—a tribute to a player.

It was during a preseason game at the Los Angeles Coliseum. Lamar Lundy, a great defensive end with the Rams, and a member of their famous "Fearsome Foursome" had been painfully stricken with myasthenia gravis, which causes deterioration of the muscles. It frequently totally immobilizes its victim and is often fatal. I didn't know Lamar had been wheeled into the Coliseum until the announcer, John Ramsey, told the fans after a scoring play that downfield, behind the western end zone was one of the greatest Rams of all times, Lamar Lundy.

When the spotlight shone on him the crowd stood up and cheered and cheered for at least five minutes. I had to hold up the game. I didn't have any control. I didn't even want it. The people wanted to give him their tribute and stopped the game to do so. A number of the players ran down and shook hands with him and patted him on the shoulders and there were a lot of wet eyes for a while in the stadium. I know that the rest of the Fearsome Foursome, Merlin Olsen, Deacon Jones, and Rosey Grier, do a lot to help raise funds for him and for the fight against myasthenia gravis. One of those programs was the L.A. Chapter of Myasthenia Gravis Foundation Salute to the Fearsome Foursome—on January 21, 1978—in Los Angeles. Lamar Lundy is on his way back—not to pro football—but to a productive life. It's a long, hard battle, but he's winning.

One of the most inspiring games I ever worked was one between the Raiders and the Chiefs, played at the University of Washington, in Seattle. The proceeds of that game were for Brian Sternberg, a pole vaulter who had become handicapped through a freak trampoline accident. During the halftime many athletes competed in a mini-track meet. Some of them talked to Brian through an intercom on the field. It was an emotional moment when Brian told them how great it was that they were out there competing for him, doing what he could no longer do.

I was in San Francisco and saw the 49ers play the Rams in a preseason game of the 1977 football season. When Joe Namath came into the game the crowd gave him a big hand. This guy was one of the greats and they wanted him to know how much they appreciated him. But you should have heard the fans cheer when he got sacked by the 49er defensive line. This is one thing about pro football that makes it different from other levels of the game. The fans can show their class for a player's ability no matter who he plays for.

Fans don't get a complete picture of Joe. His image is so often pumped out of proportion, the human side of him gets lost.

When the Jets were going to Miami to play Baltimore in Super Bowl III, he said they would beat Baltimore. Hardly anyone else thought that was possible.

The Jets had four equipment boys and when Joe walked into the dressing room the kids were packing the gear into the big trunks to go to Miami. One of the kids was in tears. Joe asked him what was wrong and the kid said,

"They're only gonna take three of us and we flipped and I lost. I can't go."

"I guess they don't understand how much the guys on the team appreciate what you do for us all year. Here," he gave the boy three one hundred dollar bills. "You get yourself a plane ticket and you come to Miami with us and keep track of your expenses and let me know if it costs you any more for the trip." You don't always hear about those kinds of things that he does, but that's the kind of guy he is.

One of my favorite football stories is about a tribute paid to Joe. Our crew had just finished working the Kansas City-Pittsburgh game on November 15, 1970, and had a two-hour delay at the Pittsburgh airport. We were sitting in the airline hospitality room, watching the Rams-Jets telecast from the West Coast. Joe had suffered a fractured right wrist in the Baltimore game three weeks earlier and was out for the season. The Jets had been struggling along ever since. Sitting with us, with a large cigar clamped between his teeth was a priest, who just happened to be six feet six and weighed about three hundred pounds. A lady came into the room and asked, "Who's playing?"

"The Rams and the Jets," someone said.

"What quarter is it?" she asked.

"The fourth," I answered.

"What's the score?"

"31-20. The Jets are winning."

"You mean the Jets are beating the Rams and they're doing it without Namath?"

"Who's playing quarterback?" her husband asked.

"Jesus," the priest said in disgust, as he stuffed his cigar back into his mouth.

You really get a feeling for the diversity in people's lives when you get to know them. It's interest in the sport which often brings them together. Ron Mix, All-Pro guard, was at a gathering to promote his team, the San Diego Chargers. He noticed a man who was sitting all by himself. Ron is a very sensitive person, and while the other guests were crowding around the football players, he went over and introduced himself. They shook hands and the man very cordially responded, "How do you do, I'm Dr. Jonas Salk." Possibly that great doctor, who is responsible for conquering polio, still gets plenty of recognition in his own time and way, but Ron said it sure seemed out of perspective for people to be praising the prowess and aura of celebrated football players in the same room with him.

Ron himself retired from football to enter law practice. "I am going to retire and go into law. So far I've made my living by charging two steps forward and hitting a guy. Now maybe it's time to do something more than that." One of the things he has done since was to represent Portland of the World Football League with player contract negotiations.

Joe Foss, the first commissioner of the American Football League, and I were coming out of Kezar Stadium in San Francisco after an Oakland Raider game. Two young kids looking for autographs of famous football personalities stopped us.

"Are you a player?"

"No," I said.

"Are you a coach?"

"No." Then he turned to Joe and asked, "Are you a player?"

"No," Joe said.

"Are you a coach?"

"No."

They both turned and ran away. Obviously we didn't qualify. I couldn't help but smile.

Joe was one of the greatest war heroes of this country. He shot down more enemy aircraft in World War II than any other marine aviator. He is a recipient of the Congressional Medal of Honor and was twice Governor of South Dakota.

I don't know about many of the contributions players

make outside the stadium, but I do know about some of them. Once, when Deacon Jones and I were entered in an Air Force Celebrity Golf Tournament in California, I was introduced to Dennis Blackman, who was on the trip with Deacon. Dennis was one of quite a number of fatherless boys to whom Deacon has offered a lot of time, support and understanding as part of the Big Brother Movement. Deacon has also given a great deal of energy as a member of the Board of Directors of the Boys Club of San Diego.

Many of football's finest devote a great deal of their time to others. I've heard several say that they, themselves, feel so grateful and so fortunate to be doing what they are doing in professional football. They feel an obligation to their fans and supporters and this is one of the ways they can express that gratitude by giving of their time and effort to participate in benefit games, speak at dinners and other fund raisers for worthy causes, as well as spending time with people less privileged than they.

Just a few years ago I had the pleasure of attending a reception in Helms Hall in Los Angeles—Citizens Savings and Loan Athletic Museum—for Floyd Little, the great running back of the Denver Broncos. He was being honored for all the help he had given to underprivileged children in the Denver area.

On the way home from the final game of the season when Rod Sherman was playing for the Oakland Raiders, we ended up on the same crowded airplane. Rod had a huge package in his lap and I asked what it was.

"I don't know," he said, "I have this twelve-year-old boy from a broken home that I sort of look out for and see that he gets to the games. After the game today, he was waiting outside the dressing room with this present he made for me. I'm not supposed to open it till I get home."

Mike Garrett and John Hadl have given their time and other valuable energies to help youth in the San Diego area.

ELEVEN

"You're the first person I ever waited to meet since I stood in line for Wendell Wilkie. I watched you referee the whole game and you were wonderful. You didn't make any mistakes. You were just great."

—*Anonymous lady*
Three River Stadium
Pittsburgh, Pennsylvania
November, 1970, after a
Pittsburgh Steeler game.

The Oakland Raiders have more fans than I do and so do the Kansas City Chiefs. The LA Rams do and so does Dallas; in fact, any team that has more than fifty thousand season ticket holders is definitely way ahead of me. I may have only a few full time fans, but they're loyal.

There was a barefoot kid who ran across the field as I was walking off Frank Youell Field in Oakland and grabbed my hat and took off with it. I chased him about fifteen yards but there was no way I could catch him. The last I saw of him he was going around the end of the bleachers. Those old AFL hats had a fancy logo on them and cost eight dollars, and to make things worse, it was the first time I had worn this one.

A police officer caught up with him, though, and brought

him to the motel where the officials dressed, about a block and half from the dressing room-less stadium. The officer had seen the kid, from the top of the bleachers, stuff the hat in his shirt and line up in front of the hot dog stand. The kid was shaking as the officer asked me if I wanted to press any charges against him.

"No, why don't you just leave him here and I'll take care of it."

The officer said, "Okay."

I told the kid that those hats were expensive and this was a new one, but if he wanted one I'd send him a used one. He gave me his name and address and when I got home I sent him one.

139

The next time we went to Oakland there was the kid waiting by the gate as we walked down the street from the motel. He said, "How do you like my hat?" It fit him fine. His mother had taken about a two-inch tuck in the back. I don't know where he is now, but I'll bet he's on the Oakland Raider season ticket list. Since then I've sent out caps to a lot of kids but none was as memorable as that first kid from the chase.

Mickey Flynn of Anaheim High School was one of the greatest runners in prep ranks durings the 1950s. Mickey told me his wife, Kathy, has a wall filled with "a whole bunch of stuff about you." She probably wants to root for the winners at every game, that's why she follows an official's career.

One day coming back from a game in Chicago a man came to my seat in the airplane and said, "My son and I were at the Bears game today. Weren't you the referee?" I told him I was, and then he asked if I'd talk to his son, who was eleven at the time. The boy came over and asked me questions all the way back to Los Angeles. He wanted a picture and I sent him one and I received a nice thank you note later.

When I retired from the NFL and became Supervisor of Officials for the short-lived WFL, I went to Chicago to be on a TV sports interview show. The kid I met on the plane, now fifteen, saw the show and took the time to write me a letter. It was nice to be remembered, even though it arrived "postage due."

You ever heard of Oconomowoc, Wisconsin? I hadn't either until Bonnie Chapman, a lady who was my secretary at the Orange County Department of Education told me about it and a young niece of hers, Andrea Beth Chapman, who lives there. When Bonnie was back in Oconomowoc on vacation she told Andrea to look for me in the TV game they were watching and I would say hello to her by pulling down on my ear. When I did, Andrea was thrilled. She went jumping all over the room. She wrote to me and asked for an autographed picture, which she keeps with her special dolls in her special closet, and charges everyone two cents a look.

Once when I was assigned a big game in Green Bay I offered to get tickets for some people in Oconomowoc, including my fan Andrea. At first not one of them believed that it was possible for me to get them into that game. They were people who had followed professional football season after season from the distance of a black and white television set and the tabloid headlines of a city's local newspaper. It was a beautiful feeling for me to make it possible to get people to a pro game who had never been to one. It was one of the few chances an official gets to be a big man.

Pulling my ear was my trademark. Yes, to the home viewing fans of pro football, I said hello and delivered other messages by pulling my ear lobe after scoring plays.

It all started back in the third year of the American Football League. One of the two family cars was in the shop, so Beth drove me to the airport for the trip to Denver, and planned to pick me up when I returned. I figured if I was lucky and could get a police escort out of the stadium traffic I could make the six o'clock plane. If not, I'd have to take the later flight. She asked me how she would know. I told her that if the first half goes according to the usual time schedule and I could arrange a police escort I would pull on my right ear lobe to let her know. "Every time one of the teams scores a touchdown, makes a conversion, or kicks a field goal, the TV cameras will zero in on me to get the scoring signal. When they do if I pull down on my ear you know I'll be on the early plane. Otherwise I'll be home late."

The police in Denver, as usual, were very accommodating and said they'd have an escort for us and the first half went along right on schedule. So, after each score I pulled my ear. Beth met my flight and it worked out fine. Well, the next Tuesday at the Kiwanis Club some of the guys wanted to know why I was pulling my ear and I told them I was saying hello to some of my friends. They thought that was really special. So from that time on whenever I had a speaking engagement I always closed by saying, "If you're watching the game this weekend and you see me, number eleven, refereeing the game, after I signal a score I'll tug on my right ear. That means I'm saying hello to you."

I got a lot of mileage out of this. One time I told it to a country club in Huntington Beach, California, on a Wednesday and on the following weekend I was on television. A member of the club was sitting in the nineteenth hole and was telling someone to watch for my signal. Well, on about the third play of the game someone scored, and I pulled down on my ear and the guy got so excited he ran into tables and knocked over drinks, pointing to the screen and telling everyone, "There he is and he's saying hello to me!"

About a half hour before a game in Buffalo, the NBC director came into the officials' dressing room with a bigger "Hello." He told us the field was too wet for the scheduled halftime entertainment, so they would like to interview me over the network stations. I said I couldn't be interviewed on television because it would be a violation of my contract. He called the league office and Mel Hein approved it.

Well, just before halftime there was a pass thrown over the middle by San Diego and a Buffalo player came up in the air and got hold of it but he never had possession and it popped out of his hands—a muff. Our umpire, Paul Trapinsky, ruled it as an incompleted pass. When a Buffalo player fell on the ball the fans thought the Bills should have been given possession, but San Diego was given the ball. The crowd booed for the last three plays of the half, and I was committed to be interviewed on TV. The rest of the crew went into the locker room.

The NBC people used a towel for me to stand on as a marker for the fifty yard line by the sidelines and handed me a microphone and put a plug in my ear so I could hear Kyle Rote who was up in the press box. During the time I was on the air—I believe it was about five minutes—there were snowballs coming from every direction and I had to stay on the towel. After the call against their team, I didn't know what might possibly be in them, especially the direct hits. I kept remembering when I was a kid in Pennsylvania, how some kids used to load them with rocks.

An unknown Buffalo player was right near me. He was in a walking cast and didn't go to the dressing room with his team because of the sloppy conditions. He stationed himself just off camera, wearing one of the heavy parkas with Buffalo Bills sewn on it, and took the brunt of the snowballs. I never found out who he was but I sure owe him a great deal of thanks.

I answered Kyle Rote's questions by ducking: "On a play like that, our field judge," and I would duck to the left, "would cover the downfield man," and I'd duck to the right. "Then he picks up the man," and the snowballs then would be flying all over me. Kyle finally stopped it, saying something referring to the heavy onslaught that was making it difficult for me and how he thought I wanted to get back to the locker room. I thanked him and ran inside to the officials' room where I let the rest of my crew know how I had taken it for one of their good calls that everyone *thought* was bad.

The worst part of it though, was that when I got home I found out that my wife, Beth, had dozed off near the end of the half and woke up at the start of the third quarter. She didn't see what I have to go through. I guess she's not my biggest fan even though I still think I am hers.

It seems traditional in baseball to boo the umpires as soon as they come onto the field. I've never been cheered when I walked into a stadium but I haven't gotten booed either. Football crowds are different from baseball fans.

I learned something else about the differences between baseball and football fans. In my Dad's last few years, he was restricted to a wheelchair because of a slight stroke. After he passed on, my mother told me, "It's a funny thing but every time I took Dad to a baseball game I pushed him all the way from the car to our seat in the stands. No one ever offered to help me. But I never went to a football game with him that someone didn't stop me and push his chair all the way to our seats. And after the game they would come back and push him back to the car. Isn't that funny? Isn't that odd?" she said.

I am proud of my fans, but even prouder of the growth of professional football—the AFL in particular. The story of the Oakland Raiders is typical of that growth. After playing their first year in San Francisco's Kezar Stadium, the Oakland Raiders moved to Candlestick Park. I refereed their first game there on September 4, 1961, when they beat Denver 49-12 before 6,300 fans. The 49ers of the NFL didn't play in Candlestick until later.

In 1962, Oakland finally got a field on their own side of the San Francisco Bay, called Frank Youell Field. I refereed the first game there, between the Raiders and the San Diego Chargers, on August 26. The Raiders lost 27-33 before 17,053 fans. It was an old recreation field and they added bleachers, and had very meager dressing facilities. As a matter of fact, the officials dressed for the game a block and a half away at a motel. We had to walk to the field, and had to have a lot of fast answers on the way back, I'll tell you.

We worked at Youell Field through the 1965 season, and they came close to selling all twenty thousand seats. Each year they were able to tuck in a few more seats. The stadium was later torn down to make more room for Oakland City College. By the 1965 season, Oakland had developed quite a following, and when they got their present coliseum built, nobody was going to be left out.

On September 18, 1966, I got the assignment to open the new coliseum when the Raiders lost to Kansas City 32-10 before 50,746. Wayne Valley was one of the Oakland owners and I gave him the whistle I used in that game.

In 1969, in a preseason game between the Oakland rookies and Dallas rookies, over 32,000 fans turned out, paying $3.50 a seat to watch. Nobody was going to be playing but rookies! The Cowboys had a quarterback who was dropping the ball all over the place that day. I thought, here is a kid who won the Heisman and Maxwell trophies when he played for Navy, but he must have lost what he had during his four years in the service. He didn't look like he could make it with the pros. His name, Roger Staubach.

During preseason training, the 1977 Raiders played near their training facilities in Santa Rosa, California, and the place was packed at $5 a ticket. Yes, football had caught on. It's hard to believe that just a few years earlier we couldn't give our complimentary tickets away. Not even to the kids walking by the stadium.

I couldn't say what city has the most rabid fans. I do know that they are different and treat the officials differently. Tickets are really important to people in some football cities. I've heard of cases where if a couple has season seats and goes through a divorce, the wife and husband get the tickets to the games split in the property settlement agreement so that each one gets to go to every other game. It may be easier to decide on who gets the house, who takes the kids, than who gets the tickets to the games.

TWELVE

Mike Garrett, the great Kansas City running back, and I were guests at a Continental Airlines Management dinner.

The last comment of his talk was, "I was in the bottom of a pile of players once, and some guy bit me. When I got up, I asked John if he saw the guy bite me and he told me he didn't see anything. John never saw any of that stuff that went on under the pile."

My opening line was, "Mike, when you're under that pile, you're on your own."

It's not so. It's just not true. I don't have any kind of contract with any chewing gum company. What is true though, is that I can't referee a game without chewing gum. If I am out there to work a game and I don't have my gum, well, they might just as well have me handcuffed. I've got to have that gum. If I don't have some there's no telling how the game might go.

In the beginning of each season I would go out and buy several boxes of gum, as it was the implied rule that I was supposed to supply everyone on my crew with some for each game. One day I passed it out to the crew and forgot to put some in my own pocket. It was a game in Denver.

I went over to the Denver bench before the game looking for their trainer to see if he had any. John Ralston, the head

coach of the Broncos at the time, came over and asked me, "What are you looking for?"

"Your trainer."

"What do you need?"

"Some gum. I need some gum."

"Just a minute," and he went over to the bench and started rummaging through equipment boxes. There was the head coach, a few minutes from kickoff in an important game, pawing through the team's accessory boxes, looking for some gum for me. What a contrast. He looked over his shoulders and yelled, "Is Spearmint all right?"

I nodded back and laughed to myself. I would have taken anything and he's asking if Spearmint is good enough. When he brought the pieces of gum over, he handed them to me, then pulled them back, "What the heck am I being nice to you for?"

I paused, as I grew one of my few smiles on the field, and said, "Because you're one of the good guys, John."

There was a time in Kansas City, later, when he would have wanted all the gum back. And, it wasn't because he needed it to keep warm because the chill factor was way below zero. It was December 3, 1972, near the end of the third quarter of play.

We had a time-out for television. The snow was in flurries. The field would change from white to raining, white to raining. It was a sloshing mess. We were standing around with our whistles hanging around our necks and our hands in our pockets.

The play after the time-out had some interest to John. People have always wondered why we stop a play after— right after—we see any kind of movement on the offensive line. Why don't we let the play finish and then give the opposing captain the choice of options for the illegal procedure foul? One of the reasons for stopping the game is that by letting the play go on the offensive unit may display a play designed to exploit a weakness they've spotted in the defense. By the time the penalty is administered the defensive scouts will have telephoned down to the sideline and the defensive weakness is corrected and the opportunity is lost.

What happened to Denver on this play was that one of their interior linemen moved before the ball was snapped. I threw a flag. My umpire threw a flag and so did the head linesman, but the play got away. Denver made a beautiful gain of seventeen yards but we had to call it back because Kansas City took the penalty. Denver was now five yards back instead of seventeen yards down the field. John was jumping around over there on the sidelines, but that was okay 'cause that's the legal "coach's jumping place."

Just a few plays later a player was shaken up and in came the trainer. Time was called and John was motioning to me, something fierce, and I figured he wanted to talk to me so I ran over and asked him, "What's the trouble, coach?"

"Why did you let that play get away? Why didn't you stop the play?"

"John, we tried. We all hit the whistle but the pea in the whistle is frozen to the side of it. It made a tiny little tweak that couldn't be heard more than two feet away. I'm sorry, but that was the best that we could do."

He looked at me, grinned, and said, "Of all things that have to happen—a frozen pea—and it had to happen to me." He was the type of guy that could go with a logical explanation even though it might kill him out there on the playing field.

In that same game there were some mixed feelings on the Denver bench about a call I made regarding Charley Johnson, their quarterback, and a fumble. He had gone back to pass and somehow he jarred the ball loose. He did it with his knee or hand and it popped out for a fumble. He had actually pulled it down. He didn't throw it and he wasn't in the act of throwing. He just pulled it down and it popped out, and Kansas City recovered it. The quarterback wanted me to call it an incompleted pass but I couldn't because it was a fumble.

When the team got back to their training facilities the following week, and were looking at the game films, they saw that the quarterback very definitely had jarred the ball loose himself. After they reviewed the play a couple of times and everyone saw that it was a fumble, John told the team and staff, "I'll tell you something. I've known that official for quite a long time, and he's one of the best referees in the business and always has been. As far as I am concerned he still is."

It's nice to hear something like that although it came to me second hand, from Dick Cory, who was an assistant for John at the time and later became coach of the Portland franchise of the World Football League. As I've known all along, I wasn't out there to get standing ovations from coaches, but when you've retired from the game, the more confirmations you get about the good ones the less remorse you have to feel for the few that got away.

One of the most beautiful moments I have ever witnessed in sports happened in that same game between Kansas City and Denver. Towards the middle of the fourth quarter, with less than ten thousand fans left in the freezing stands, Denver running back Floyd Little made a long gain. There was a pileup of players where he was tackled.

Floyd screamed and I knew immediately that he was hurt. He was bent over backwards with Kansas City linebacker Jim Lynch underneath him. His legs were pinned down and the rest of the pile of players were twisted around him like a tight-fitting sculpture. It didn't take a Michaelangelo to carve away the humanity to get to him, but the art of unpiling over an injured player requires moves just as delicate.

Jim yelled, "He's hurt. He's hurt. I'll hold him until you get everybody off. Everybody included such light and tender pieces of humanity as giants Buck Buchanan and Curley Culp. Their hearts were even bigger when they got up. Those two Kansas City players carefully carried Floyd to the Denver sidelines, and wouldn't come back onto the field until they knew the doctor was taking care of him.

After I retired I spoke at a clinic with John Ralston. He told me and the coaches there how the finest act of sportsmanship he had ever experienced was the time Floyd was carried off by the Kansas City players and how Coach Hank Stram was out on the field that day even before him. The incident fully crystalizes my contention that the game is not a manhunt, but a game which can bring out the best in men.

Since that clinic I have spoken with John about the need

to reduce the friction that exists between coaches and officials.

John has suggested that there be a clinic where officials and coaches meet in an attempt to improve the quality of communications between them. Something that might lessen the negativity that is so much a part of the lifestyle of coaching staffs on the sidelines of Sunday football. I have tried with high school coaches and officials to have these kinds of meetings, but unless it is mandatory the coaches will not show. And when I have gone to talk with various teams, professional, high school or college, all the teams have asked that I keep my talk short. Twenty minutes at the most. They just didn't have the time. Maybe coaches' and officials' clinics could overlap by one day and that day be spent working on more positive attitudes between them.

Coach Ralston's suggestions have to do with what he refers to as "improved attitude control, more effective communications, and better interpersonal relationships." I don't think it would do anything but help the league if officials and coaches had a chance to have group meetings, with film sessions, to discuss and analyze each other's performances. Such meetings would convince coaches they don't need to "bait" or to try to put fear into officials, in an attempt to influence their decisions. I wouldn't even be surprised if some coaches feel they have to psych out the officials as much as they have to psych up their players.

Hank Stram deserves a hell of a tribute for what he did in Super Bowl IV. Not only did he lead his team—the Kansas City Chiefs—to victory in the game, he allowed himself to be wired for sound. I don't think too many coaches would grant the public such a privilege. He probably thought it would be good for football, as it would give the fans an inside look at what goes on during a game among players, coaches and officials.

During the game the coach was upset because he felt we had missed a foul he had seen, and he started blasting, "How could they do that? How could six officials do that? There's six of them out there and they missed it. Not one of them caught that!''

Tommy Kelleher, a top NFL official, was working on the Kansas City sidelines and heard Hank. As Tommy got closer to where Hank was standing, Hank walked out on the field and yelled something like, "Hey, Mr. Official, what's going on?"

Tommy was astute enough to know that there was no way he could possibly explain to a coach during the middle of a Super Bowl that someone could possibly have seen the play differently than he did. So, he just listened as Hank went on and on. Finally he turned his head a bit towards the coach and told him very congenially, "Hey, coach. You're on the field."

Immediately you heard Coach Stram say, "Oop," and he jumped back off the field. Tom had jarred the coach's mind enough to get him off the subject as well as off the field.

A few plays later though, there was a measurement right in front of Coach Stram. I remember this quite well. On the television you could hear the voices, but all you could see was a crowd of ball players.

The coach was saying, "We made it. We made it. We have a first down!"

And then another voice came in, mine, "Hold it, you haven't made it yet. Stretch out the chain." There was a kink in the chain and someone was standing on it. We pulled the chain out tight and they had made it by about two inches. "Now you've made it." I told everyone.

"That's great! What a great job of officiating. How about those guys. Aren't they doing a great job out there." So Hank sounded good through most of the game. The final score was 23-7, so he looked good too.

I have been asked many times if I have ever been involved in a protested game. The only "sort of" protested game I was associated with was between the Kansas City Chiefs and San Diego Chargers. The reason I call it a "sort of" protest is that I've never heard of a protest being upheld in pro ball.

The game was about eight minutes old when a TV time-out was taken and San Diego Coach Sid Gillman called me to the sidelines. When I went over to him, he told me, "That player, number 65 on Kansas City, is illegal. He doesn't have a contract on file in the league office."

I said, "I'll check it out," and ran across the field to Kansas City coach, Hank Stram, and asked him if that were true.

He said, "No, that's not right. We sent in his contract Friday, and the confirming telegram, too. That makes him eligible."

I ran back across to the San Diego side and told Coach Gillman. He replied, "Go tell him we're playing the game under protest."

So I ran back across and told Hank Sid was playing under protest. He said, "Go tell him where he can stick his protest."

I replied, "That message you can deliver yourself, Hank. I'm getting tired of running back and forth across this field. What the hell do you think this is, Western Union? I'm going to start up this game again so I can get some rest."

To this day I never heard any more about the protest. I think the three of us were the only people who knew about it.

I was attending an educational meeting in New York during the Super Bowl II week of 1968. The meetings ended on Wednesday and I took a couple of days vacation and flew down to Miami for the game between Green Bay and the Oakland Raiders.

After checking in Thursday morning I called Mel Hein. We had lunch and he gave me tickets to some of the social events prior to the game. One of them was a dinner for several hundred people hosted by the Miami Dolphins.

I went to the banquet and as soon as I walked in the door I ran into George Wilson, the Dolphin coach. He asked me where I was going to sit and when I said I didn't know he invited me to sit at his table.

When we all rose for the invocation, the reverend father asked a blessing for the Green Bay Packers and the *San Diego Chargers* instead of the Oakland Raiders. Hundreds of people were choking back a laugh and I whispered to Coach Wilson, "He blew the prayer."

George replied, "Yeah, I wonder how much the Chargers and Sid Gillman had to pay for that."

One summer the AFL office called and asked me to contact Sid Gillman and set up a time for me to go to the San Diego Chargers training camp and talk to the team on rules. While I was there Sid started to discuss some of the San Diego games I had in previous years.

I told him, "Sid, one of these days we'll both retire and the two of us will go somewhere, get a bunch of sandwiches and beer and go over all the calls you ever questioned. All of them." I have retired, but the trouble is Sid just keeps on coaching.

Sid was a great one. Sometimes he would ride you all during the game for what he thought you should have called but every once in a while he'd admit that he was wrong.

Frank Kirkland called a clipping foul in a game with San Diego and Sid got on him for it. He didn't realize at the time that the call had been made away from the place where he and the rest of the crowd were looking. On the way out at halftime Sid said to Frank that he'd check his film and if that was a clip he'd buy him a steak dinner. Well, a couple of weeks later we were in Denver for a game with San Diego and the first thing Sid said when he saw Frank come on the field was, "I looked at my films and I guess I owe you a dinner." The dinner wasn't important but it was mightly nice to know that Sid was big enough to admit it.

Sid wasn't as benevolent a couple of weeks later, right

before a game in Buffalo. It was one of the early AFL games between the Chargers and Bills. The rain and snow didn't seem to know how to stop. A drastically miserable day.

When I got to the field I discovered that the grounds-keepers had left the tarp off the field the night before. It was a sea of mud. Sid was fit to be tied. He said it was a disgrace to good football players to make them play in such conditions, and suggested that I forfeit the game to San Diego.

"Hold it, Sid. We've got a big network commitment, and I am not taking any kind of responsibility for calling off a game. If you want me to I'll call the league office to try and find someone who will give me the authority to call off the game, but I can't take it upon myself to do it."

Sid laughed and then told me that he had already called the office and they had said the game wouldn't be called off.

"Would you have let me forfeit the game, Sid?"

"No, of course not. I wouldn't have put you in a spot like that." But the way he winked at me when he said it, I wasn't too sure what he would have done. I don't think he would have but I am glad we didn't have to test it.

When Tom Fears was the head coach of the New Orleans Saints he brought them to the San Diego area for their pre-season training camp.

Fears and Sid, who was still with the Chargers, arranged for a practice scrimmage and contacted me to get some officials to supervise it. I got hold of Aaron Wade, Barry Brown and Frank Kirkland and asked them to come with me.

In such a scrimmage penalties don't mean much. After every three downs the ball automatically goes back to the thirty yard line. Within the first few minutes of the game one of the Saints' defensive ends was clipped. We threw the flags but the players wanted to retaliate. We pulled them apart and encouraged them to get ready for the next play. The next play ended with the San Diego player, who made the clip, on the ground. The Saints player came running over to him to continue their disagreement.

Coach Gillman must have thought the coming player was going to pile on his prostrate player so he dashed off the sideline to stop him. The big end ran right into Sid with a forearm to the jaw and Sid fell like he had been hit with a Colt 45.

Insulted and probably embarrassed, Sid got up and demanded, "That's all. This scrimmage is over. We came to play, not to fight."

Tom came running over. "Come on, Sid. Let's get on with the practice. I'll send my man to the showers."

"No. It's off. We're going in."

"Tell you what. Why don't each of you fine anyone who throws a punch five bucks a throw?" I suggested.

They both laughed, and Tom said, "Five dollars! You got to be kidding. We fine a guy more than that for losing a jock strap." But they both agreed, so I called all of the players together and told them, "The next time anyone starts a fight, two things will happen. One, we don't stop it, and two, everyone who throws a punch will pay five dollars for every punch."

"Hell," one of the players said, "no punch is worth five bucks." That settled it. There were no more fights the rest of the afternoon. I am sure Sid's jaw was sore as hell when he read about it in the next day's sports section.

When the American Football League started, Sid Gillman gave the league some advice that turned out to be a solid foundation for the new league. "Let's develop our own stars," he said. He believed it would be foolish to spend a lot of money trying to entice stars to leave the NFL. He felt we should sign good college seniors and in a few years they would become true AFL stars. With few exceptions that is what happened.

I couldn't help but remember Sid's words fifteen years

later when the World Football League started and spent huge sums of money on established NFL players. Perhaps if they had spent the money more wisely the WFL would still be with us today.

THIRTEEN

Question: What were your biggest thrills as an official?

Answer: Super Bowl IV and the longest game

SUPER BOWL IV

"You've got the big one, head mother," Bob Baur, my field judge, called from Ohio to tell me during the Christmas holidays of 1969.

"Who told you? How do you know? They haven't contacted me about it."

"I just found out. Congratulations!"

"Now don't start kidding around about something like this."

"I am not. You're the referee for the Super Bowl. Don't tell me you're the last one to find out about it?"

"Listen. A few years ago a couple of guys started calling

HELPING THE RUNNER

some other officials and told them they had the Super Bowl when they didn't. The guys told them that they weren't chosen for the play-off games because they were being saved for the big one. And it was damn cruel when they found out they didn't get it.''

Bob told me who was on the crew, and said, "I am not kidding you. Good luck.'' One of the men mentioned was Bill Schleibaum who lived in the Los Angeles area. I called him and he said he hadn't heard anything either. In a couple of hours the Western Union office phoned with the news. They read it to me and said they would have it delivered but I said, "No thanks. I am coming to get it myself.'' The big Christmas gift had come and the whole family started jumping around like a bunch of little kids in a pregame huddle. I was assigned Super Bowl IV, in New Orleans.

The crew was a mix of AFL and NFL officials. From the AFL there was me as the referee, Harry Kessel, the head linesman and Charlie Musser, field judge. From the NFL there was Lou Palazzi, umpire, Bill Schleibaum, line judge, and Tom Kelleher, back judge. Bob Finley of the AFL and Fred Silva of the NFL were the alternate officials. I wrote to all of them and asked them to be ready to talk to the rest of us about their positions and how they liked to work. The game would be the last time two *true* NFL and AFL teams played against each other for the world championship. The following year everyone would be under one banner—the NFL.

The pregame meeting with the people from CBS was so detailed and involved with what they wanted the officials to do, that I thought that I was going to be paid a talent fee from the network for working the game instead of as an official from the league. The pregame meeting on Saturday, with just the officials, had a lot of tension until I deliberately started calling everyone by someone else's name. When the supervisor of personnel, Mark Duncan, came in, I introduced him as if no one knew who he was. Everyone started to laugh and the pregame adrenalin was lowered.

He was joined by Mel Hein, the Supervisor of Officials for the AFL and Art McNally, Supervisor of Officials for the NFL. They talked about the two teams in the game, each from their respective leagues. Mark and Art spoke of the overall play of the Minnesota Vikings—insights into their style of play, plays they might run, ways they might line up and what we could expect when they were in certain formations. Mel did the same thing about the Kansas City Chiefs. Nothing was mentioned about specific players.

I talked about how I wanted the chain brought in and how I liked fouls reported to me. I wanted them reported by color and number. Some referees like to have the other officials report to them by stating whether it's the offense or defense, and the number of the player, but what I wanted to hear was something on the order of HOLDING on 58, BLUE.

The commissioner's office felt there would be a lot of noise on Bourbon Street the night before the game, so we were assigned rooms on the top floor and at the back of the hotel, out of the way of the partying. The pregame celebration in the city was so wild that Beth and I decided to find a more quiet and unspontaneous setting—a movie, "Hello, Dolly."

I don't know what the players were doing the night before the game, but I slept soundly. Beth was mad with envy because she couldn't sleep, worrying about how I was going to do the following day.

When I awoke it was raining hard. I wondered later why I didn't get depressed thinking about how the game I had waited twenty-five years to officiate would be played against the elements more than the teams against each other. As I looked outside I thought about how I would have to watch the finest athletes in the country, slide, fall and stumble with the ball popping and slipping to and away from them. We were told the day before that the field was covered, but that didn't matter now. There would be no tarp on top of the grass keeping the water out. Beth assured me that it would be clear by game time. I don't know how she knew but she knew—the sun came out a couple of hours before kickoff and the day was beautiful.

Because the parking facilities were sparse around the stadium Art McNally drove us to the ball game. I learned later that the Kansas City Chiefs' police escort didn't show up when the team wanted to leave their hotel for the stadium, so their bus left without them. They had to talk themselves through various security points along the way. (Imagine the Super Bowl as an intersquad game among the Minnesota Vikings? Sorry, fans, but there will be no refunds.)

The first foul called in the game came when Minnesota punted to Kansas City early in the first quarter. Fred Cox, the punter, got the kick away but when he did, four Chiefs were all over him. As I was walking off the penalty, and getting ready to give the Vikings another first down, Hank Stram was telling his players what a stupid mistake like that had cost the team.

On my game report card where I recorded the fouls and offenders, I put down "Roughing the kicker—front four— take your pick." You are allowed to touch the kicker if you hit the ball, but they missed it so they weren't allowed to come in there and level him like they did.

Tommy Kelleher, our back judge, came up to me after the play and said "Good call, John. That set the tone for the game."

For the most part he was right. When the kicker started off the field in the direction of the Kansas City bench I slipped up behind him and said, "Go to your left." He was probably looking at all four sides of the stadium at the same time. Thank God he didn't have to kick again, soon.

Kansas City was a surprise team to make it to the Super Bowl for they had finished second in the AFL Western Division. But they beat favored New York 13-6 and Oakland 17-7 in the play-offs, and weren't favored to win this game either. Minnesota's record was very impressive. They had lost only one game during the season, and beat the heavily talented Rams before coming to New Orleans.

I like Bud Grant's observation, "Defense wins football games. Offense sells tickets." He had the men to back up that statement in one of the most respected defensive lines in the game. Kansas City's defense was bent upon keeping Joe Kapp from getting out of the pocket and using the ends for double teaming. It was a well fought contest up in the trenches—the front lines—however, the Chiefs' front line gave Dawson enough protection to work away from the oncoming "purple gang."

The turning point of the game, I felt, came when Kansas City scored to go ahead 16-0 in the second quarter. Kansas City had just kicked off after their third field goal and the Minnesota receiver couldn't keep control of the ball and lost it on a fumble to offensive lineman Remi Prudhomme. The ball was placed on the Minnesota nineteen yard line. On the first play Dawson was dropped for an eight yard loss. Wendell Hayes then blasted through the left side of the line for thirteen yards. A pass to Otis Taylor was good for ten yards and the Chiefs found themselves on the four yard line, first down and goal to go. Mike Garrett lost a yard on the next play and then was held for no gain. With third and five the "65 toss power trap" play was called. Here is how it looks diagrammed in football art.

16 Len Dawson
21 Mike Garrett
71 Ed Budde
76 Mo Moorman
77 Jim Tyrer
84 Fred Arbanas

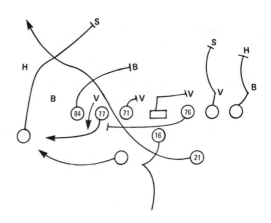

Hank Stram said, "It's a play we had for sometime, but we didn't use it until this situation. Our tackle (Jim Tyrer) pulled to influence his man (Alan Page). When Page came through he was open to the inside-out trap made by the right guard (Mo Moorman). It also took a good block by the tight end (Fred Arbanas) on the middle linebacker, and we got that."

Mike Garrett, who scored on the play, said later that it was the type of play you look "awful foolish on if it doesn't work."

Garrett was so elated over making the touchdown that he rushed back through the pack toward the bench and ran smack into me as I was coming up to spot the ball for the extra point.

Both teams scored touchdowns in the third quarter but the game was out of reach for the Vikings. Minnesota got one penalty in the fourth quarter that hurt their cause. It was a late hit on Len Dawson, the Chiefs' quarterback. Just as Len rolled over and looked up to say something about the foul, my flag was flying right under his nose. It was fifteen yards for roughing the passer. He said, "Well, all right" and got up and ran to the hash mark. I got the players up, picked up the ball and started marching off the penalty.

Later I found out that Len was under more pressure than just the game. He had taken a lot of verbal abuse and innuendo during the week prior to the game from the media, regarding an investigation made by the Department of Justice. It was about his "supposed" associations with an illegal gambler. It was all disproved.

I felt even sorrier for Minnesota quarterback, Joe Kapp, after his last play of the game. The Vikings' last chance to win had slipped away and Joe just sat there on the field amid the blood, the mud and the dejection, frustrated from the day's work.

The game wasn't a difficult one to work. The great teams don't get to the Super Bowl by committing a lot of foolish fouls during the season. They play the game like they're supposed to. It's a tremendous responsibility for officials in a game of this magnitude, but the job itself isn't really difficult. I only called two fouls all day.

There were no complaints from either coach afterward. In fact, during the game there was *less* than the usual amount of negative comment from the sidelines. The players played the game and let us run the game. There were few rule changes to adjust for the game. The AFL's two-point conversion rule was tossed out for the game and the official time was kept by the scoreboard operator, not the back judge, as it was done in the NFL. Both offenses used their league's ball.

I don't know what the best play of the game was but it might have happened before the game started. A football fanatic from California flew in for the game. When he got into the stadium and found he had forgotten his whiskey he left to go to a liquor store. Another car was blocking him and when he went to push it out of the way himself, five guards grabbed him and put him in a lockup outside the stadium for the entire game. It turned out he had been trying to move the governor's limousine. But he was alive and well into his cups when he introduced himself to everyone on the plane back to LA.

The Tuesday following the game I was at my Kiwanis Club meeting and was introduced by Ken Lloyd, the President, who said, "Here is a guy who directed a game that half of the population watched. He had more control over what went on last Sunday than anyone else in the country. We watched him more than we would have the President of the United States." They gave me a standing ovation.

About a month after the game I was playing in a golf tournament in Palm Springs and my partner on the second day was comedian George Gobel. We got around to talking about the game and I told him I was paid fifteen hundred dollars for working it. He said I was grossly underpaid for running one of the biggest shows in the world. That I had more attention focused on me in those three hours than any other segment of television and that I should have been paid forty or fifty thousand dollars, "at least." I asked him if he wanted to be my agent, but he said, "I work alone, I'm a monologist."

The game meant a lot more to me than the fee I received. It was the end of the AFL. I was proud to be the only man to start and finish the league working at the referee's position. I was there at the beginning and I was there on the final play when the league came to a successful end. All the old AFL teams are now in the American Conference of National Football League.

THE LONGEST GAME

For the gift of a pro football play-off game to come up on the television set on Christmas Day somebody had to spend the night before in a big city hotel far from his home. Make that at least eight officials, not to mention the players and other team personnel.

The coffee shop is closed, so is the newsstand and gift shop. The three bellmen who are doubling as elevator operators all lost the flip of the coin that decided who would work the night shift. Everything is so still and somber that you go up to your room and think you'll find some solace in some food sent up from room service. You get the hotel operator on the phone who tells you that the kitchen won't be opened until the day after Christmas, but suggests "There's a little hamburger stand that's open two blocks up the street."

And when you walk up there the thought of eating isn't enough to forget the fact that you'd rather be going home with the people in the street, who are hurrying with their packages for the evening festivities.

I got a hamburger anyway, and when I got back to the hotel began calling around the city looking for a restaurant for the rest of the crew. There were eight of us because in 1970 a play-off crew consisted of six regulars and two alternates. A few days before Mel Hein had phoned and told me, "We've been talking back here and just realized that you guys will be alone in Kansas City on Christmas Eve, and the commissioner told me to tell you to take the crew out to dinner, to the best place in town, and put it on your expense account."

There wasn't much open, but we finally found a place, thanks to Jack Fette, an official who lives in the Kansas

City area, but wasn't working the game. The bill wasn't even seventy dollars for all of us and when the office got my expense account in the mail Mel telephoned me and asked, "Where did you take those guys, McDonalds?"

"No, but you didn't want me to run up a big tab, did you?"

"We told you to take them to the best place in town."

"That was the best place that was open within a fifty mile radius of Kansas City."

Not only was it the longest and loneliest night for a life-time but the game the following day, Christmas 1971, was the longest football game in National Football League history. It was the Miami Dolphins against the Kansas City Chiefs and at stake was the chance to play for the American Conference Championship, which was the final ticket to the Super Bowl.

In the first quarter the Chiefs completely dominated the Dolphins by shutting off fullback Larry Csonka and picking apart the Miami zone defense with short passes and occasional traps and draws. The Chiefs were ahead 10-0 going into the second quarter.

Bob Griese connected to Paul Warfield and Marv Fleming while Kansas City was concentrating on the Miami running game, and Csonka plunged in from the one yard line for Miami's first score. Kansas City running back Ed Podolak fumbled which set up room for Miami kicker Garo Yepremian to boot a field goal and tie up the game before the half. From what I understood after the game, Garo Yepremian had been upset that Jan Stenerud, the Kansas City kicker, had been voted the American Football Conference's kicker in the Pro Bowl, and that that had given him extra incentive to outperform him.

With Miami's defense keying on Kansas City receivers Otis Taylor and Elmo Wright, the Chiefs had to resort to more of a running game. Podolak became the main man in the offensive concept of Kansas City that day, accumulating 350 of the Chiefs' 606 yards, passing as well as running. Miami's attack was more diverse. After Kansas City went ahead on a Jim Otis one yard rush for a touchdown, Jim Kiick scored for Miami after passes to Howard Twilley and Warfield. It was 17-17 going into the fourth quarter.

After a long bomb from Len Dawson to Elmo Wright and a three yard run by Podolak, Kansas City led 24-17. Griese came back with the Dolphins mixing it up again with short passes, a reverse, a draw and a sideline pass before connecting with Fleming on a hook pattern in the end zone for a 24-24 ball game with 1:36 to play.

Kansas City had another chance to score after a long punt return by Podolak but Stenerud missed a game winning field goal and the contest went into overtime. One overtime wasn't enough. There were two before the game was completely over. In the first, both Stenerud and Yepremian missed crucial kicking attempts for a three point victory. In play-off games you don't stop at the end of the one overtime; you keep on playing until one team makes any kind of score, touchdown, field goal, or safety, and then the game is over.

It seemed quarterback Bob Griese had only one play left in his repertoire for the last quarter. It was what they call in football parlance the roll trap that goes against the flow. Kiick and Griese would start to the right with Kiick running behind Csonka. Griese would then hand the ball off to Csonka and he would get good lead blocks from tackle Norm Evans and guard Larry Little. It worked well enough to get the Dolphins down in the Chiefs' thirty-six yard line. On a fourth down Yepremian came in and kicked the ball through the uprights for a field goal. Eighty-two minutes and forty seconds after the opening kickoff I raised my hands to signal that the kick was good and the longest game in all football history finally came to an end. Miami 27-Kansas City 24.

With all the excitement about the length of the game and the importance of the play-offs themselves, not many people remember one of the most dramatic elements of the entire show. On the last play of the regulation fourth period, Miami kicked from behind their own goal line and the ball was caught sixty-three yards away. Kansas City had twin safeties; one of them signalled for a fair catch but the other man caught the ball. A fair catch gives you two options if the man who signals for it is the man who catches the ball. You can take the ball, first down and ten providing there is still time left in the game, or line up for a free kick, like a kickoff, where the teams are ten yards apart and the kicker can make his kick without being rushed until his toe touches the ball. If the ball splits the uprights it counts three points. If the other guy signals for the fair catch, the team does not have the field goal option.

I think Coach Stram thought he could try the field goal option and, if successful, end the game right there because when I got to him on the sideline, he asked, "If we kick it, can they return it?"

I answered, "Yes but——." Before I could remind him that his player who caught the ball was not the one who signalled, he saved me the trouble.

He looked down under the Miami goalposts and there was one of the finest kick return artists in the league, Mercury Morris, pawing the turf. He thought about this for a second and then turned to his field goal kicker, Stenerud, and asked, "Can you kick it sixty-three yards?"

"There's no vay, coach," Jan answered in his soft Norwegian accent.

Hank looked at me and said, "All right, the hell with it. Flip the coin."

The flip was for the beginning of the first overtime. The rest is history.

FOURTEEN

The World Football League—

From a wonderful dream—
To a bitter disappointment—

Twice.

A few days after I retired from the NFL, I received a call from Gary Davidson, the president of the World Football League. He wanted to know if I would be interested in helping them with their officiating program. I had known Gary for several years and was familiar with his talent of putting a league together, but I was a bit dubious about anyone taking on the NFL. However, another longtime friend, Don Andersen, had just given up one of the best public relations jobs in the country at the University of Southern California, to join the WFL and that made me feel confident the new league could make it.

I told them that I would only be able to spare enough time to conduct two clinics and assign and give limited supervision to the officials since I was still the Assistant Superintendent

of Schools for Orange County. This was satisfactory to them. Gary told me he had just hired Henry Lee Parker, who had been the player personnel director of the New Orleans Saints, to be the Director of Football Operations. He asked me to come down to the WFL office and see Parker. Their office was only a few minutes from mine so I drove down during my lunch hour and met Henry Lee.

Five minutes after we met, Henry Lee pulled a huge cardboard carton from a closet. It was overflowing with queries, resumes, letters of recommendation and photographs. They were all from prospective officials and he asked me if I would put them in some kind of order and grade them. I was shocked. It was late March and they planned to start playing on July 10.

I took the box home and Beth and I spent every night and the entire weekend sorting and compiling all the applications. I graded them into four piles marked: Hire, Acceptable, Maybe, and No. The next morning I took them down to Henry Lee, and he said he'd get to work on it. He asked me if I knew any of the applicants personally. I had seen or worked with ten of them. They were Barry Brown, Hunter Jackson, Tommy Miller, Aaron Wade, George Kennard, Bill Summers and Bill Wright with NFL experience. Les Bruckner, Don Berberet and Mel Ross worked local college games. Henry hired them all.

A few days later Henry Lee called to say he was going to take a trip East and South and he would interview and hire the rest of the forty-two officials I said we needed. He was about to hang up and I asked, "Henry Lee, what about the Rule Book?"

"Oh, you're supposed to write that," he replied. "I'll leave a memo on it for you. See you in a couple of weeks."

To save time I dropped by the office and picked up the memo. There were six changes from the present pro rules that they wanted incorporated into a *WFL Rule Book* by May 1, five weeks away.

I spent every night, every weekend, and my entire Easter vacation on it. About the end of the third week I read in the paper that Tom Fears, the coach of the Southern California Sun, in Anaheim, said he liked the new rules. He mentioned four I had never heard of. I got ahold of Henry Lee, who was still in the East, and he had never heard of them either. It was next to impossible to reach anyone at the league office because everyone was frantically running all over the country trying to tie together all the loose ends by kickoff time on July 10. Finally, I got Don Andersen, who said, "Oh, those, they adopted them at the end of a league meeting about three weeks ago." I had to write them into the book, which meant every page had to be double checked because football rules are always cross-referenced to each other.

Henry Lee returned from his trip a few days later and I told him that there were a number of things that needed approval from the rules committee. He got up, walked to the door, closed it and returned to his seat. He smiled and said, "O.K., John, the WFL rules committee meeting is now in order. What do you want approved?" The two of us decided what we wanted the rules to say.

We had a total of thirteen rule changes to open up the league:

1. The kickoff was from the thirty yard line, to encourage runbacks.

2. The goalposts were moved from the goal line back to the end line to discourage field goal kicking.

3. A missed field goal kicked from outside the twenty yard line was returned to the line of scrimmage. A kick missed from inside the twenty was a touchback. This rule also discouraged field goals.

4. The receivers had to touch one foot inbounds for a pass or an interception to be complete, instead of two.

5. Offensive backs could be moving toward the line of scrimmage prior to the snap.

6. A fourth down pass, incomplete in the end zone, would be awarded to the defense at the previous spot rather than the twenty.

7. Offensive holding was reduced from fifteen to ten yards.

8. The hash marks were moved in seventy feet from the sidelines.

9. The fair catch was not permitted. However, the players of the kicking team had to stay five yards from the receiver until he touched the ball. Any of his

teammates who were in the five yard restricted area could not block for him until he cleared the area.

10. The offense had twenty-five instead of thirty seconds to snap the ball.

11. An eligible receiver could be bumped once within three yards of the line of scrimmage. After that he could not be bumped anywhere.

12. If a game ended in a tie, a complete fifth quarter was played, broken into two seven and a half minute segments. If it was still tied or had been retied at the end of the two segments it went into the records as a tie.

13. The kick for the point after touchdown was eliminated. Instead the touchdown counted seven points and the ball was placed on the two and a half yard line. If the team passed or ran it into the end zone it scored one point, which we called the "action point."

Of the above rules, numbers 2, 3, 6, 7, and 11, are now used all or in part by the NFL.

Of all the rule changes we made, the action point created the most excitement. In game after game the final score was in doubt because of the possibility of a made or missed action point. It was only successful about sixty percent of the time instead of about ninety-eight percent for the kicked extra point. The idea of the action point was the brainchild of Bill Finneran, a systems analyst from New York State. He had figured out how few times the colleges and the old AFL had used the option of running or passing and the percentages of success. He concluded that it was a risky play and the great majority of coaches avoided it even though it counted two points instead of one.

Finneran made the proposal to the league but his suggestion was that the ball be placed on the two yard line. They asked me what I thought of the idea and I said I liked it but I wrote across the proposal, "Why not put the ball on the three yard line instead of the two?" I just wanted to make it a little tougher. The owners adopted the rule at their next meeting but they couldn't get ahold of either of us to find out why he wanted it on the two and I wanted it on the three. So, they did the all-American thing and compromised, so the action line became the two and one half yard line.

Somehow the rule book got written, Henry Lee hired the officials and I held my western clinic in mid-July 1974 in Santa Ana. The following weekend I held a clinic for the eastern and southern group in Memphis, Tennessee.

During the western clinic one of the young attorneys from the league office came up and handed out the travel cards. Someone asked, "What class do we travel?"

He asked how the NFL officials traveled and was told first class.

"O.K." he said, "First class, we're just as good as they are."

I couldn't believe it and asked Henry Lee. He checked it out and said it was okay. I fully expected to have the men go coach for the first two or three years just like we had done in the old AFL. Each week I would be sending thirty-six men flying all over the country, including ten home games in Hawaii. The difference between that much first class and coach travel was a financial burden a young league should avoid.

We were to play on Wednesday nights, with a single nationally televised game on Thursday night. All twenty weeks' games counted in the standings.

When I saw the schedule I asked about the final ten weeks' Thursday TV games which were not listed. I was told that they would announce them later in order to take advantage of the best matchups. I felt this was an extremely serious mistake because season ticket holders would have their game date and starting time shifted at the last minute. It proved to be a valid concern. Twice in the final ten weeks the games at Anaheim were changed from 8:00 P.M. on Wednesday to 6:00 P.M. on Thursday. The paying fans indicated their displeasure by staying away in large numbers.

On July 10 we went to Birmingham for the first game between the Southern California Sun and the Birmingham Americans. I was amazed to see a near-sellout crowd, but I was even more amazed when the team came on the field. The fans stood and cheered for ten minutes. They hadn't played one play and already their fans loved them. Birmingham won 11-7. The league was off to a great start.

The next morning we flew to Jacksonville for the first nationally televised game. There we were met by a group of dignitaries and all the media people. They took us to the Sharks' offices for a reception and I was awed by the luxurious suite of offices. I remember thinking, "These people must have an unlimited supply of money."

That night almost sixty thousand people jammed the Gator Bowl to see the Sharks beat the New York Stars 14-8. The other games that week were Portland at Philadelphia, Hawaii at Florida, Houston at Chicago, and Detroit at Memphis. We had a fantastic opening. The NFL players were on strike and we would be playing for four weeks before the NFL got started, if and when they got the strike settled. The TVS Network billed us as "The Only Game In Town," and we were.

All the hectic exhausting work had been worthwhile. If anyone had said the league would be broke by the end of the season he would have been labeled as stark raving mad. But then things started to go bad.

The financial picture of some of the clubs started to turn sour and they came to the rest of the league for a loan. But, when the other clubs loaned them money, they too got into financial trouble.

When it came time for the clubs to send in their payments to operate the league office, they were late and then soon defaulted so the whole league operation became troubled.

The Philadelphia Bell had attendance figures of 55,534 and 64,719 for their first two home games. The Memphis Southmen and Birmingham Americans became natural rivals overnight and drew 61,319 to their first game.

But when coach John McVey took his Southmen to Philadelphia on the fifth week, only 12,396 paying customers showed up. There had been rumblings that the Bell had "seeded" their first two games with free tickets. "Papering the house," is not new in sports or entertainment, but this time it backfired. The press played up the "WFL paper scandal," and the league lost a big part of its credibility.

At the end of the eleventh week, the Houston franchise moved to Shreveport, Louisiana. The thirteenth week, New York moved to Charlotte, North Carolina. The next week, Detroit and Jacksonville folded. The rest of the clubs hung on for the full twenty weeks, but Chicago forfeited their final game to Philadelphia.

The first and only World Bowl was played in Birmingham on December 5, 1974, before 32,376. The Americans had a 22-0 halftime lead and then had to hang on tooth and nail to outlast the Orlando, Florida Blazers 22-21. After the game the sheriff confiscated the Americans' uniforms. Each winning player got twelve hundred dollars and each loser, eight hundred and fifty.

What had started out with such bright beginnings had turned into a bitter disappointment in just twenty weeks— what happened?

Probably the thing that hurt us the most was the inability of the New York Stars to find a place to play. Yankee Stadium was expected to be under repair for two or three years and the Yankees and Mets and Jets had Shea Stadium booked solid. The Stars had to settle for a dimly lit field on Randalls Island, just across the Little Hell Gate Channel from the sewage disposal plant. The only way to get there was over the Triborough Bridge. An 8:00 P.M. kickoff on a week night meant bucking the tail end of the rush hour in order to make it. After the game there was another traffic fight to get home by midnight. It was too much trouble and the people gave up after a few tries. The Stars gave up too and moved to Charlotte.

When the team left New York the league was in big trouble. In order for a professional sport to succeed it must have a franchise in New York City. New York is the sports switchboard of America. No longer were we "where it happens," we were out in the hinterlands trying to "make it happen."

When John Bassett, who could afford it, signed Larry Csonka, Jim Kiick, and Paul Warfield, of the NFL Miami Dolphins, to 1975 contracts, prior to the start of the league in 1974, it gave the WFL instant credibility. But, when the rest of the clubs started to put out or encumber large sums of money for NFL stars, I remembered what Sid Gillman said about developing our own stars when the AFL started in 1960.

By necessity, Gary Davidson and his corps of vice-presidents had to be traveling almost constantly. At first Gary wanted to be known as the league president but a few weeks prior to the opening that was changed to commissioner. There were hundreds of items that needed decisions and the men in charge were almost impossible to reach. I felt that Gary should have been president of the WFL and run the board of governors and big policy, but that someone, preferably a football man like Henry Lee Parker, should have been the commissioner, who stayed in the office and run the football program.

About the ninth week of the season, Henry Lee Parker was made the Vice-President for Football Operations. This gave me a great feeling because now Henry Lee would be there to give immediate answers to football questions, telephoned in daily, by football people. We would have a knowledgeable football man who was not in competition calling the shots on football people who were in competition with one another.

But, at the end of the eleventh week the Houston Texans moved to Shreveport and became the Shreveport Steamer. Problems arose and Henry Lee had to go to Shreveport to pilot the Steamer that was running aground regularly. In his absence, here I was, a consultant on officiating, not being paid nor wanting to make management decisions, but being called by junior executives and secretaries asking me to do just that. After a while, coaches and general managers of the clubs would call me direct because they could get ahold of me. Needless to say, Henry Lee and I ran up quite a telephone bill between Shreveport and Santa Ana.

On Monday of the eighteenth week I flew to Chicago to cut some television commercials for one of the sponsors of the Chicago Fire. When I finished taping, one of the sportscasters told me there was a big meeting at the airport hotel and it looked like Gary Davidson was going to be ousted as league president.

I went out to the hotel and saw Gary sitting alone in the press room. He said things didn't look good. I told him to hang on because I felt sure the owners would not overlook the fact that he and his staff had been working twenty-four hours a day, seven days a week and sleeping on airplanes to keep things going. Nobody could have worked any harder than Gary. On October 29, Gary Davidson resigned as president of the World Football League.

On November 22, Chris Hemmeter, a co-owner of the Hawaiians, was named the new president. Hemmeter said the league had huge financial problems but he felt they could be solved. He listed the most important assets of the league as quality performance on the field, TV exposure in a hundred cities, and the league structure including the league office, public relations and publicity, rules innovations and the officiating.

Near the end of the season some of my officials reported that the airlines had refused to honor their travel cards. I was told that this was just a temporary thing and new money was coming. We asked the officials to pay their own travel and expenses and they would be reimbursed at the end of the season. The way it turned out, none of them got paid for the final three or four games and they did not get reimbursed for their travel or expenses. I didn't get paid for the final month of my service.

After the season, rumors flew thick and fast. One day there would be a report of new financing indicating that all bills would be paid. The next day we would be told that everything was lost. Each time I stopped by the league office there were fewer and fewer people and more and more empty offices.

The officials would write me and call and I tried to keep them informed. I sent out dozens of letters to all forty-two men and made countless telephone calls at my own expense.

There was no way Chris Hemmeter or Don Regan, the league's legal counsel in Newport Beach, could tell me anything other than that they were trying to save the league. Finally, the league started bankruptcy proceedings. It had lost twenty million dollars.

Meetings followed and Hemmeter traveled thousands of miles to try to build a new league out of the ashes of the old WFL. In the early morning hours of April 16, it was announced at the Waldorf-Astoria Hotel in New York, that there would be a World Football League in 1975. Chris Hemmeter would be the president. It would be known as, "The New League, Inc.," doing business as the World Football League. Certain considerations were made to the "old WFL" for the use of their name, their logos, and their player contracts.

Probably the best explanation was the notice that appeared at the top of the records section of the *1975 WFL Media Guide;* it said:

ATTENTION:
Last year's statistics and records are being entered here as a service to the media who may

> *be interested in the continuity of such records. It should be noted, however, that last year's teams played for what is now legally known as the Football Creditor's Payment Plan, Inc., formerly known as the World Football League, and now in Chapter Eleven reorganizational proceedings. This year's World Football League is a completely separate and distinctive league, even though some players and franchise locations are the same as the "old" World Football League of 1974.*

On May 16, I received a telephone call from Hemmeter's secretary in New York. She said that he wanted me to be at the league meetings in Birmingham, Alabama, over the weekend, and to be ready to meet with the rules committee. She said I should see Frank Sanok, the Vice-President for Finance, when I arrived and he would reimburse me for my transportation. I wasn't too sure I wanted to risk any more of my money on an airplane ticket, but I wanted to make every effort for the forty-two officials who had given up their college careers to turn pro, so I bought the ticket and went to Birmingham. As soon as I got there Sanok paid me for my trip and told me to sign for my room and food at the hotel.

Then I met Chris Hemmeter and found him to be energetic, personable, and an astute businessman. I told him that I was going to retire from public education on June 30, and would devote my full time to the WFL. I said I needed the title of Supervisor of Officials and had to be in total charge of the officiating program, answerable directly to him and the Vice-President for Football. I assured him we would have to give each official at least a five hundred dollar expense advance before any of them would take a step outside their door to go on an assignment. He agreed and we worked out the terms of a three year contract for me.

The only restrictions Hemmeter put on me was that I had to keep the officials' travel to a minimum. I explained that the only way that could be done was to hire some officials in Hawaii, Portland, and San Antonio to augment the group we had in 1974. We would have to give up the set crew concept and have the men work several times close to home.

We shook hands and he told me, "I think you should know that you will be the only person on the league office staff who was with the league office last year."

Our meeting was followed by a press conference where I was introduced as the Supervisor of Officials. I stayed for about thirty minutes and then went to my room and called my seven referees and told them to call their crews and find out if they wanted to continue. By 11:00 P.M., I reported to Hemmeter that thirty-nine of the forty-two men would be back with us.

The next morning I met with the rules committee and within two minutes they all agreed that they wanted to eliminate the use of the "Dickerod," a device to replace the rods and chain for measuring for a first down. We had to use it in 1974, because of a marketing agreement. It had moving parts and would malfunction. The coaches didn't trust it and it drove the officials wild.

The other rule changes we adopted were:

1. The tie breaker was changed from the two seven and one half minute segments to one sudden death overtime period, where the first team to score is the winner, providing both teams have had an offensive opportunity.

2. On all kicking plays there was no blocking below the waist. This eliminated the blind-side cut-down block at the player's knees.

3. A kicking tee was allowed on field goals as well as kickoffs.

4. The penalty for an ineligible receiver downfield was reduced from fifteen to ten yards.

Financially, the league would operate under the "Hemmeter Plan," which made all the players shareholders in the operation. If a game was a sellout they got a healthy paycheck. If the gate was small they would be paid a minimum fee.

The new WFL was made up of the Birmingham Vulcans, the Charlotte Hornets, the Chicago Winds, the Hawaiians, the Jacksonville Express, the Memphis Southmen, the Philadelphia Bell, the Portland Thunder, the San Antonio Wings, the Shreveport Steamer, and the Southern California Sun.

The best news of all was that the Chicago Winds expected to sign Joe Namath within two or three days. If this were accomplished a lucrative television contract was assured.

The league was split into Eastern and Western Divisions and there would be a summer and fall season. The six teams that were the division winners in each season would be in the play-offs.

The Birmingham meeting ended on Sunday afternoon with everyone extremely excited and optimistic. This time we were doing it right.

A few days later it was announced that Joe Namath had decided not to sign with Chicago. It was a blow that we felt we could overcome. However, we soon got a more serious setback when the TV contract failed to materialize.

I hired fifteen new officials and held clinics in Youngstown, Ohio; Victoria, Texas; Memphis, Tennessee; Portland, Oregon; and Honolulu, Hawaii. All the officials paid their own transportation and expenses at the clinics. They wanted the league to succeed and were willing to help.

Chris Hemmeter set up the league office in New York City and put Mike Martin, a brilliant young sports executive, in charge. Mike and I became good friends via daily telephone calls.

The first thing I asked Mike to do was send out a letter to all the owners and coaches explaining that due to the very tight budget restrictions we would not be able to move the officials around the country. Therefore, the same men would work a number of their home games. We further told them that they should refrain from using "hometown officials" as an excuse for a loss on the road. This was an admonishment some coaches proceeded to totally disregard. The press had a field day talking about "home cooking."

The play of our teams was better than in 1974 and it looked like we could make it. Most of the clubs had TV coverage going back to their hometowns when they played away and the press was beginning to notice us. But, attendance started to drop off.

On September 2, Hemmeter announced that the Chicago franchise was revoked due to inadequate financing.

On October 1, I flew to New York to visit the office and then went on to Philadelphia to interview and observe some prospective officials. On October 4, I attended the San Antonio at Philadelphia game and there were less than three thousand people there. The press gave it little or no notice before or after the game.

I was interviewed on San Antonio TV at halftime and the item the sportscaster wanted to talk about most was why we kept our officials so close to home.

On Monday, October 20, I got a call from Martin. He wanted me to come back to New York in about ten days, prepared to give the owners a complete plan, including costs, for putting the officials in crews and moving them around the country as in the NFL. They said they wanted to do it the next year.

On Wednesday, October 22, I was working out at the Santa Ana YMCA when I was called to the telephone. It was Beth; she said, "Call Mike in New York, it's urgent."

I called Mike and he said, "John, it's all over. The league has folded. We'll make the announcement in about an hour."

I notified the officials but this time they got paid in full for the games they worked and they all actually returned the unspent portions of their expense advances.

What happened the second time around?

The league went for twelve weeks but the attendance had declined twenty-eight percent during the final five weeks. We couldn't recover from the backlash of the first year. When Joe Namath decided not to sign with Chicago it caused the TV network to withdraw their offer, so we were at the mercy of the gate receipts. Once again, the man in charge, Chris Hemmeter, had to fly back and forth between Honolulu and New York and there were several times that Martin and Sanok told me they needed his immediate persuasion and clout to keep a club from making a foolish move. But Chris was in the air. Most of all, though, we couldn't regain the credibility the "old WFL" had lost in 1974.

For the second time we went from excited optimism to bitter disappointment. There would not be a third time.

Was it worth it?

Yes, I think it was. Everyone I've ever talked with that was a part of the WFL remembers the hurt of it but they all agree it was a great adventure. They made many lifelong friends and have memories enough to last forever. A great many players and coaches had a showcase they wouldn't have had any other way.

The next year, in 1976, one hundred and forty-four players from the WFL beat out NFL players for their jobs. Twenty-seven coaches moved into the NFL. Two of them, John McVey and Jack Pardee, became head coaches.

It was probably the most exciting, challenging, frustrating, scrambling, never-know-what-will-happen-next time of my life. But, I'm glad I was part of it.

FIFTEEN

Fathers and Brothers—
Mothers and Sisters—
Uncles and Aunts—and——
Cousins—

"Now stop to think about it, mom. That kid playing against your son has got a mother sitting over there on the other side of the stadium, and she's bleeding on every play just like you are. And she wants her son protected just like you want your son protected.

"She doesn't want your kid to do anything foul or illegal to gain an advantage over her kid. So, when you get up to scream at the officials for calling something against your kid, remember, that the official may have called a penalty on someone else's kid a while back, trying to protect your son."

I explain this to mothers at high school booster club meetings. For probably the first time in her life, "mother" has to sit up there in the stands and watch some other kid belt the

hell out of her own kid. It's a pretty traumatic experience for most parents. What I want them to understand is that each kid is out there trying his best to make the kids on the other team look bad. Officials are just out there to make sure that game is played fair and to assess penalties when someone makes a mistake.

In 1955, the principals of the twelve high schools in Orange County, California, asked me to be their area commissioner, to assign officials for their football, basketball and baseball games. A job I have been doing out of my home ever since. The list of schools and sports has grown. Today, I do the assigning for sixty-five schools in nine sports in Orange County.

As high school commissioner you get called upon to help deny what mothers don't want to believe. I was speaking at a banquet and a mother stood up and raised her voice. "My son was given an unsportsmanlike penalty for using extreme profanity during a game. Now, I'll have you know that my son never swears."

My hands were tied. What am I going to tell her, standing there in front of two hundred people, most of whom were parents of ballplayers? If I told her the truth, she would be embarrassed and so would everybody else. I simply said, "Well, somebody out there was swearing and unfortunately the referee or some other official must have thought it was your son."

She sat down, contented, no longer feeling guilty for having a kid who went out there and said what was really on his mind.

I've only thrown a few players out of football games for using extreme profanity in the time I've worked as an official, and every time, somebody would show up the next day trying to convince me that the player was an "altar boy."

In the early 1950s I was working a high school game at Citrus College in Azusa, California. About five minutes before the end of the game a kid about 6'3" and weighing about 225 pounds slugged a player on the other team. I flagged him down and *ran* him, which means I threw him out of the game.

After the game my crew and I were in the locker room when a man about 6'4" and weighing about 250 pounds came in. He was wearing a tan camel's hair overcoat, a felt hat, and had about an eight-inch cigar stuck in his mouth. He spoke in a rasping guttural voice, "Which one of you guys threw number 56 out of the game?"

Before I had time to identify myself three of my crew members were already pointing at me, saying, "He did." The man, stepping over all the field equipment on the floor, walked over to me.

"I am his father."

I thought, "Oh, hell. Here it comes." He stuck out his hand to shake, and said, "I want to thank you, 'cause I can't do anything with that big oaf. It's about time somebody straightened him out."

My chin fell in amazement, but I shook hands with him. Then he took us all out to dinner to celebrate what he felt was his son's growing-up party.

I worked a Santa Barbara-Occidental game as referee when my nephew, Roy Gaebel, was playing for Santa Barbara. Normally, you are never assigned games in which relatives are playing. In this situation, I was asked to be a last-minute replacement for an official who had the flu.

In the second quarter, Roy was standing deep in his own end zone, getting ready to punt. The snap from center came high and he leaped up to catch it. When he came down his back foot landed on the end line. I hit the whistle, raised my arms over my head with my hands together, in the signal for a safety. Two points for Oxy.

He turned and asked, "What's the matter?"

"You're standing on the end line. That makes you out-of-bounds. It's a safety."

"You technical bastard," he exploded.

"Your mother is my sister. If I am a bastard, what does that make you?"

He tossed me the ball with a smirk on his face. "You're funny, too, Uncle Jack." I learned quickly about genetics and athletics—when you're an official even your relatives hate you.

When my son, Joel, was a quarterback at Santa Ana Valley High School, his head coach, Dick Hill, called me and asked if I would get some officials to work a pre-season scrimmage for him. I got a couple of men and went over to the school.

On the second play, the defense put a blitz on and I found myself chasing right along with him. I was ignoring everything else to protect my son.

Right then I knew why no league wants to assign officials to games in which their children or other relatives are playing.

People have asked me on many occasions what I think of kids' sports, such as Pop Warner, or Jr. All-American Football, and the Little League. They are always surprised when they find out that I am not in favor of them. Highly organized sports can do a lot of kids a lot of harm.

First of all I don't think that many kids can handle the competition at that age and I am quite sure that many of the parents can't handle it either. Years ago, a friend of mine, who was umpiring a junior league baseball game called a kid out on strikes. When the next kid was up to bat, my friend was down on one knee looking at the next pitch. The father of the kid he had just called out came up behind him and slugged him across the back of his neck with a bat. The father was beside himself later and couldn't imagine what he had done, but the umpire was in a brace until the next season.

Parents become too protective of their children. They empathize with them so they can't stand anything that seems to hurt them. Their egos get damaged if their son looks bad in front of everybody else.

In another junior league contest, the umpire was so appalled by the language of one mother, that he went over to her between innings and said that he would appreciate it if she would tone down her language. "After all, these are just nine and ten-year-old kids."

"Well, you can go straight to hell," she told him.

At the end of the next half inning he was brushing off the plate when somebody tapped him on the shoulder. He turned around to face her husband who looked like a pro wrestler. "Nobody tells my wife what she can and can't do. When this game is over, I'm going to clean your plow."

The umpire told me that he casually walked down the third base line while the pitcher was warming up, got his keys out of his pocket, took off the big pillow protector from his chest, and hollered to everyone, "The game is over," jumped into his car and left.

I have visited a number of parks where young kids are playing in the junior leagues. The pep talks some of the adults give to kids would make you physically ill. The way they harangue them and make themselves think that they're getting kids psyched up is inhuman. If a high school coach talked to his team the way younger kids have been "pumped up" players wouldn't play for him and school principals would want his dismissal. Coaches of young kids' teams somehow get away with incredible abuse.

Coaches that demean kids are only trying to alleviate the frustrations they had as players, or to soothe their egos over the fact that they thought they could coach on a more sophisticated level, but never got the chance. So, the kids are the ones who catch it.

A number of young athletes play such high-pressured ball that by the time they get to high school, they don't want to play in any kind of organized school sports. Last year, a third of our sixty-three schools cancelled their junior varsity or sophomore football schedules after the season started. These weren't high schools with two or three hundred students, either. These schools had enrollments numbering close to two thousand.

When I talked to some of the athletic directors at the schools, they hinted or told me outright that many potentially good athletes had learned to hate the game. When you hear an adult screaming at you, "I want you to hit that other guy until it hurts. I want you to destroy him," how can you expect anyone to grow to love the game? Kids who went out and hurt their own muscles and emotions for mom, dad and the coach, weren't ready to do that again when they got old enough to make their own decisions.

I had a father come to me with his son when I was working at the Orange County Department of Education. He was concerned that his son wasn't playing football.

The boy was built perfectly to be a middle linebacker. The father said the boy went to a local school, whose coach wouldn't allow him to go out for the team because he had missed spring practice.

I went into another office and called the coach. He told me that he wanted the boy to play but that when the kid brought back the papers signed by his parents, giving permission for him to play, he told him that he didn't want to play. One of the assistants had said that it would be tough for him to make the team because he missed spring practice, but if he worked hard he could still make it. The coach said he wanted him on the team, but that if the kid didn't want to play then there was no need for him to be out there. The coach said that the kid took the papers, thanked them and left.

I went back to my office and suggested that I talk to the boy alone. I asked the father to wait outside. When the father left, I asked the kid why he didn't want to play. "Well, my father has had me playing this game since I was eight years old and I never liked it. It used to hurt and I was always a big kid and kids would bang on me. The coach always made me the tackling dummy, and he was always screaming and cussing at me. But my father thinks it's the greatest thing in the world. He just can't understand why I am not gung ho about being a football player."

"Why didn't you tell him? Why did you lie to him about spring practice?"

"Because I don't want to hurt him."

"What you're saying to me is, you love your father and you don't want to hurt him?"

He nodded his head.

"And you're not going to hurt him by lying to him?"

He nodded again.

"Don't you think it would be better if you leveled with him and told him the whole story?"

"It would be, but . . ."

"Do you want me to tell him for you?"

"Yes, I guess so, he would listen to you. That would be the best thing."

The son went out and the father came in and I told him that his son wasn't playing football because he didn't want to play football, he hated the game. Not because of the coaches or any other reason.

"What do you mean he doesn't want to play football? He was one of the best players in every junior league he has ever played in."

"But, you've been forcing him to play since he was eight years old. He just told me that he hated the game. . . The people who coached him on the lower levels did a great job of teaching him to hate the game, and I am afraid you're not going to be able to get him to like it now."

"Then why didn't he tell me that?"

"He loves you and he didn't want to hurt you." There was a pause for a few seconds and then I asked him, "Do you play any sport yourself? Like golf?"

"Yes."

"Well, why don't you take him along sometime, and start forgetting the football." I don't know whether I helped them or not, but when I saw them walking outside in the parking lot, the father had his arm around his son's shoulder.

Another element that doesn't set well with potential high school players is that they won't get as much recognition playing in high school as they got when they played in the junior leagues. There aren't as many praises and prizes in high school as there were when they were younger. In southern California schools a high school athlete is ineligible if he has received an award worth over ten dollars for playing.

If there is any kind of solution, it is probably that young kids should play more for fun rather than in highly organized levels of play. Teams with an overexaggerated emphasis on winning, and the thinking of the opponents as the enemy is a concept in life a youngster doesn't need. Some of the pro linemen I have watched play treat each other nicer than some of the kids I've seen play in the junior leagues.

Most importantly, though, for any kind of competitive sports for kids, is to keep the parents out of it. Nothing is wrong for them to be supportive from the sidelines, but when they have an identity crisis when their kid doesn't make it to second base, or doesn't throw the ball far enough to make it to the finals of the all-star, all-world nine- and ten-year-old competition, then who needs to have parents, or the game?

Nothing is wrong with making mom and dad wait until you get into high school before they join your first team's booster club. I guess what I'm trying to say about keeping the whole thing in perspective is best articulated by this invocation given by the late Dr. Blake Smith, prior to the Texas vs. Baylor football game in November, 1953.

Dear God:

It is clear that Thou has given us life with many different shades and colors. For this we are grateful. We humbly accept the fact that some things in our lives are not very important. They are to be enjoyed but not taken too seriously. The occasion that brings us together today is one of those happy interludes in life. Help us to accept it as such.

In Thy presence we know that no issues of great importance are going to be settled here this afternoon. No souls are going to be lost or saved by the final figures on the scoreboard. No great cause is at stake. It is one of those plea- sures which Thou has meant for Thy children to enjoy. Do not let us spoil it by forgetting that it is just a game to be enjoyed today, talked about tomorrow, and forgotten the day afterward. Keep us mindful of this, dear God, for we are human and we easily lose our perspective and allow the things that are most important to become the victim of the things that are least important.

SIXTEEN

A day does not go by when someone doesn't call to ask me something about football. These are not calls in the middle of the night from irate coaches and fathers, in violent protest over unbearable and impossible officiating, just the questions and answers that have gone on during my time as an ex-NFL official—

Question: Do officials have any kind of idea who is going to win a game or how close the game is going to be?

Answer: Officials, as a rule, usually have one stock answer for that kind of question. If I knew who was going to win I wouldn't be out there calling the fouls. I'd be at the betting window.

Question: What was the toughest game you ever officiated?

Answer: The New York Jets vs. the Kansas City Chiefs, on December 22, 1963. It was so cold that my lip froze to the whistle. I pulled the skin off when I pulled the whistle away from my first tweet. For the rest of the game my lip throbbed every time my heart beat.

CLIPPING

Question: Over the years, how has football changed?

Answer: First of all, football is like society in how it has adapted to specialization. Increased specialization on the field has meant that players only work one position. A quarterback used to kick, pass and run. Now, some of them only pass or hand-off. A lineman used to play both offense and defense. Now he plays either offense or defense. There are no longer general practitioners in football. Everyone has been relegated to one function.

In some respects football is also like a war. A war that has been brought down to scale so that the people can watch the teams fight over real estate. In the tenth or eleventh century it began as a kicking contest. A bladder of a pig or cow was kicked between two towns. Young and not-so-young guys would get out there and fight all day trying to kick it to the other town's steps. Somebody said that looks like fun to watch, but we can't be chasing them all over the countryside. Let's make it a game that we can sit and watch. And so there was soccer and rugby. America developed its "playing war" from them.

In American football you've got the guys up in the trenches. The men who play on the line. The guys involved in the individual fights. A lot of people come to games just to see them go at each other. They're the infantrymen.

Each side has their tank troops that come in and bulldoze over and capture real estate. The aerial corps plays up in the air in ballet dances, trying to come down with more land.

Each side has its own defense. The general staff is over on the sidelines with the general intelligentsia up in the stands calling down information to them. Spies are viewing the game for next week's wars.

All of these elements are going on and the people watching the game are fascinated by the entire show.

Football and the hoopla connected with it seem to me to answer a need the American people have for a national ritual of semireligious rite. Taken as a total, from the pre-game ceremonies to the postgame ceremonies, everyone, players, coaches, cheer leaders, song leaders, musicians, the press, and the officials, act out their respective roles with great seriousness. It must be awesome to someone who sees it for the first time.

Unfortunately, in the last ten to fifteen years, some coaches at all levels have decided that the way to play this "war game" is to teach their players to hate and maim their opponents. They do a terrible disservice to the game.

Question: How do leagues weed out officials? Why aren't you still officiating?

Answer: When an official's eyesight starts to go bad, or his legs start to leave, he'll be weeded out. They let officials go every year when they can't cut it any longer. In the college ranks, age fifty-five is the mandatory retirement age. The NFL doesn't have that ruling but if one of their officials can't make the moves any more, they'll soon replace him.

I resigned, but chances are I got out before they caught up with me. My knee hurt and I was gimping around on the football field. When I saw myself in the films I knew I wasn't doing the job well enough any longer. I could see that my crew was starting to cover up for me. They were fulfilling their responsibilities and some of mine. The knee was slowing me down and after a few films with me in "low efficiency" I decided it was time to go. Maybe if I hadn't decided to hang it up I would soon have gotten a call from the league office telling me I was going anyway, and I wouldn't have blamed them. Nobody ever got treated any better than I did by the American and National Football Leagues, I'll guarantee you.

Question: Which sports have you refereed and are there any you wouldn't want to work?

Answer: Besides football, I have refereed basketball and umpired baseball on the high school and college level. I also refereed some Navy boxing shows during World War II. I would not care to work ice hockey because the players carry clubs, and the officials aren't allowed to. I think that's kind of unfair.

Seriously though, I don't think I would care to work soccer because soccer seems to build great frustration as the game progresses.

It is extremely hard to score in soccer. As the game goes on the frustration of the players and the fans mounts and mounts, because the players get so close but can't seem to score. As the game frustration builds the players become desperate and finally one of them gets careless and commits a major foul and the referee awards a "free kick on goal" to his opponent.

The kick is good and the final score is 1-0. Then everyone blames the referee and wants to punch him out.

Question: Which do you think are the easiest and toughest sports to work?

Answer: I've worked three. From easy to tough, I'd rank them, baseball, basketball and football.

To me, baseball is the easiest to work of the three. In baseball, the nature of the game keeps the players separated. The left fielder doesn't suddenly get involved in a play at first. The play goes with the ball and you watch it and when it is over you call it safe or out. If you have followed your proper mechanics you are in proper position waiting to make the call. The major league umpires are masters at this. There are other calls such as fair or foul, ball or strike, interference or obstruction, balk, hit batsman, infield fly, a missed base, and many others that can get hairy at times. But even with a two-man crew, compared to football and basketball, the game requires little running on the part of the officials.

Another thing about baseball is that the only real penalty, other than the penalties for obstruction or interference, is to throw a player or manager out of the game. You don't have technical foul shots like in basketball or yardage penalized as in football. Wouldn't it be interesting if a baseball umpire could move a base runner up or back a base or add a strike or ball on a batter everytime the manager came out shouting?

Basketball, to me, is much easier than football. In basketball the physical beating you give your knees from thousands of trips up and down the hardwood floor means you'll have a relatively short career, and that is physically and psychologically tough. The fans who sit a few feet from you can get emotionally high and make it difficult, but that shouldn't bother a good official.

Here's something to try at the next basketball game you attend. There will be a foul called and a lot of the fans will start to boo. Look at the pie-shaped wedge of fans in the stands directly behind the official who made the call. You'll be surprised. More times than not, they are not affected one way or another about the call, because they saw it from the same angle as the official. Remember, the mechanics of basketball officiating put the official in the best spot to view the game.

In basketball you keep up with the action and when you see a foul, you hit the whistle, put your clenched fist in the air and point to the player who fouled. Then you assess one or two shots and the game goes on. That's not all that difficult. The closeness of the crowd and the physical demands, however, make basketball a hard game to work but I don't feel it is as difficult as football.

In football you have twenty-two highly spirited athletes running around and knocking each other down on one and a third acres of turf, and depending on the level of play, four to seven men are supposed to see everything they do. Now that's highly improbable, so a rather complicated set of officiating mechanics is used to coordinate each official in the best position to cover the action. This requires a lot of running.

Each man has key areas that he looks for when the offense sets its formation. He then makes an automatic adjustment and picks up his key as the ball is snapped. For instance, the tight end usually tips what kind of a play is coming in the first two or three steps he takes.

Let's say it is third and ten and the Red team is on offense and a yellow foul marker goes down. You see the official who made the call run to the referee and tell him something. Here's a sample.

"I have number 68, Red, holding, on the line of scrimmage, before the pass was thrown. The pass was incomplete." Immediately the referee's computer-like brain starts to process the information, according to the 107 pages of the rule book, as he calls for the captains. He'll then give the offended team captain these options, "You'll have the ball here fourth and ten or back there third and twenty."

If the ball is within field goal range, the captain will probably take the down over to move them back ten yards, but if it is forty yards or more away he'll probably refuse the penalty, take the down and force them to kick.

Just before the referee talks to the captains he'll flash a quick "holding" signal to the press box so the game announcer, and radio and TV people will have a moment to get ready. Then, after the captain takes his choice of options, the referee will come out in the clear, turn on his microphone and say, "Holding, 68 offense," and give the down. Then he faces downfield, raises his hand, sounds his whistle and chops his hand down. This is "declaring the ball ready for play," and the field judge starts the thirty second count. The Red team has thirty seconds from then to snap the ball or they'll be assessed a five yard delay penalty. Although there is a visible thirty second timer on each end of the field in the NFL, the field judge times each play with his stopwatch. In college and high school games they are only allowed twenty-five seconds to get the ball in play. Just as the teams line up, the linesman counts the players on the offense and the back judge counts the players on the defense. If either team has twelve or more on the field at the snap it is a foul.

All the officials pick up their key and the next play is under way. This happens, on an average, about 160 times each game.

Sounds simple doesn't it? Well that's just a very slight scratch on the surface of what each of the seven men does on an NFL crew on any given play.

Question: Were you ever physically threatened by any player or stadium filled with fans?

Answer: No. I think it's because they respect the objectivity and honesty of the officials.

Question: What happens if the officials don't show?

Answer: The game isn't played. Players have got to be protected and that's one of the big reasons why we're there. I know of some high school games that were delayed because the officials were held up in traffic and I can't remember any of the teams wanting to go on and play the game without them. Ask any player at any level and he'll tell you there is no way he'd play without us.

Question: Don't you think if there are enough blatant mistakes by officials in a game that the game should be played over?

Answer: No. To my knowledge there has never been a game replayed. What one side would call a blatant error, the other side would say was a great call. I'd like someone to show me all the games, or even the one game that got ruined or lost, or whatever, by an official's mistake.

Once in several hundred games the officials might lose a down to a team or give a team an extra down. About thirty years ago there was a college game in the East. I've forgotten who was playing, but one of the teams got an extra down and scored the winning touchdown on it as the clock ran out. No one knew there was an extra down until they looked at the game films. The team that "won" requested that the score of the game be reverted back to whatever it was before the last score. That final play really never happened, so, their team lost the game instead of winning it. The commissioner of the league didn't take the action, the team itself did. If the extra down happened earlier in the game I seriously doubt if anything would have been done. The natural tendency of everyone is to say that what happened in the last minute or so of the game was what did or did not cause the final score to be what it is. Fouls called then are the greatest target for controversy.

I've read about games in newspapers where someone on the team said that the penalties really cost us the game. Later in the article it mentioned the five turnovers and three missed field goal attempts, the four fumbles and seven interceptions, but not one wants to give those statistics as the possible reasons why the team lost. They want to believe, "The turning point in the game was when the officials called two straight penalties on us in the last quarter."

Well, the turning point for a team that thinks like that might be when they showed up at the stadium.

Question: Can a game be protested?

Answer: A coach or a school administrator can call up a league commissioner and complain or verbally protest a game but nothing is going to be done about it.

I've never heard of a protest of a college or professional game being upheld. Baseball managers go out there and yell and scream and declare that this game is under protest. If their team wins, they never file the protest. If the team loses a protest can be filed but nothing is really going to be done about it to change the score of the game. Usually what happens is that after the situation has been reviewed, everybody finds out that it wasn't a mistake at all. That someone wanted to apply a half of this rule and a half of that rule to make it come out like they want.

The only way you can protest a high school football game in southern California is if a team uses an ineligible player, which is easy to adjudicate—they just forfeit the game. Other than that no game can be protested on any official's enforcement of a rule.

Question: I remember seeing you on a close-up during a game and you were taping up a player's jersey. Why didn't you just make him leave the game?

Answer: That was during an Atlanta-New York Jets game played in New York on November 25, 1973. Oddly enough, the play involved a simple snap from center but it caused a lot of interest because it was covered so minutely by the cameras.

The game was close, so any score could later prove crucial. The Falcons had the ball deep in their own territory and on a third down play their center had the shoulder of his jersey ripped away, exposing the shoulder pad and clavicle guard. The clavicle guard is about the size of a large slice of French bread. I have seen one go right between the bars of a player's face mask and shatter his nose.

The possible danger of this is classified as "equipment that becomes illegal through play," and I could have sent the center out until it was corrected. However, what went through my mind was, "It is fourth down and Atlanta will be punting from their own end zone, and it is a wet, muddy field, which makes the snap very difficult."

If I had sent the Atlanta center out, I would have put them at a disadvantage, so I chose to use the part of the rules that permits the referee to allow three minutes to repair equipment that becomes illegal through play. I called the Atlanta trainer onto the field and the two of us taped the jersey together.

The center then made a perfect snap to the kicker who got the punt away. After the play the TV cameras followed the center off the field and the wet tape was coming off and waving in the wind. When I got home, Beth told me that the TV announcer said, "The tape job the referee and trainer put on him didn't last very long, did it?"

But, it lasted for one play, and it prevented a possible injury. It also kept the competition fair, and that was all I cared about. By the time the Falcons went on offense again an equipment boy had gone into the clubhouse and returned with a new jersey for the center.

Question: Why doesn't the Hall of Fame at Canton, Ohio, honor college players?

Answer: The Hall of Fame at Canton, Ohio is strictly for pro football.

The National Football Foundation and Hall of Fame, Inc. was founded in the mid fifties and is dedicated to the upgrading and perpetuation of high school and college football in America. After twenty years of hard work, the foundation had the grand opening of their Hall of Fame at Kings Island, near Cincinnati, Ohio, on August 3, 1978.

Each year, since 1957, the Foundation has awarded $1,000 scholarships for graduate study to the top scholar-athletes of the nation's college football teams.

Each local chapter has an annual banquet where they honor their local scholar-athletes. To be nominated by a school, a boy must have been all-league and have a grade-point average of 3.0 or better.

I feel very proud to be a charter member of the organization, and urge anyone interested in college football to join.

Question: Are you ever afraid of being injured when you are out on the field?

Answer: You don't have time to be afraid. You've got so many things on your mind during a play you couldn't possibly worry about getting hit by anyone—the players or the fans. The players do all they can to stay out of our way. I've had players hit their own men and push them out of the way in order to avoid us on the way to an opponent.

When the game film showed me being narrowly missed by some big defensive lineman, who just veered off at the last fraction of a second I'd say a little prayer of thanks, and go on with the rest of the movie.

Question: Do you ever fear any kind of reprisals from fans you've left bereaved for calls you've made during a game?

Answer: No. I'd like to meet any bereft fans. Send them over and I'll explain that a football is a prolate spheroid eleven to eleven and a fourth inches long and it takes funny bounces.

Question: Are officials manipulated by coaches?

Answer: Some coaches try to manipulate officials by intimidation; others try being patronizing, but it's to no avail. A good official is only amused by it.

Question: What do you consider a flagrant foul?

Answer: A flagrant foul is a vicious act such as a slug, a vicious clip, or a vicious grasping of the face mask. It usually carries disqualification plus the yardage penalty. The captain of the offended team may refuse the yardage, but the player who committed the foul is still disqualified.

Question: Do coaches teach their players to deceive officials?

Answer: I don't know any coaches who would deliberately teach something illegal. Many of them will take all the advantage the rules will allow though.

Question: What was the biggest error you ever made as an official?

Answer: About twenty years ago, in a high school game I allowed one team to have a fifth down and they scored a touchdown. No one knew about the fifth down at the time but they discovered it later in the film.

Question: Have you ever been mistaken for a player and been tackled or found yourself in the middle of a pileup of players?

Answer: I haven't been mistaken for a player since I played at Stanford. Seriously, it's never happened to me. Interestingly enough, that's why officials wear plain knickers with no side stripes, like the players have. We wear striped stockings that are worn with the stirrups showing like baseball players. This is done so that a lineman or other player about to block or tackle will hopefully know that we aren't one of the boys.

Question: What effect does complaining by coaches from the sidelines have on you as an official?

Answer: None, because we usually don't hear it. Many times a player or coach will put on a big show of disagreement with the officials. I hate to think they are doing it consciously but I often get the impression that they are unconsciously trying to shift the blame for a foolish foul or coaching error onto the officials.

The coach will always have the last word in a situation like this because he'll sound off and the press will print it. We won't talk to the press because we would have to point out the poor play or coaching errors of the participants. We just don't feel this is something we want to do. So we let them pop off and have their say, report the facts as we see them to the commissioner, try to make any corrective adjustments we can learn from the game, and get ready for next week.

You can hardly blame coaches for going off like a rocket when some guy in a zebra shirt sees a clip and calls it, nullifying the coinciding touchdown. Without the release of yelling at an official, the coach might go stark raving mad.

Question: Do you think that officials should be fined for making bad calls, calls that cause a team to lose a game?

Answer: Maybe the team that lost should fine the official and the team that won should pay him a bonus for making the bad call. To answer this another way, I feel that if an official consistently makes bad judgments or mechanical errors, the commissioner should drop him from his list of officials.

Question: Who decides if a player is legally on the line or in the backfield?

Answer: The head linesman and line judge are standing on each end of the line. If a flanking player wants to know if he is on the line or in the backfield and he asks an official, a good pro official will tell him, "I am on the line." If he were to answer the player, "Yes, you are on the line," or nod his head to tell him so, then he would be coaching not officiating. The accepted way is for the official to declare to whoever asks that he is on the line. The player will make his adjustment from where the official is standing. Some high school officials get themselves in trouble in this area because they are so anxious to please coaches that they volunteer to tell kids when they are or are not on the line. I've seen officials actually physically move the player up or back when they should be letting the kid do his own moving. The official can really get into trouble if the player is moving when the ball is snapped. If the player is illegally in motion the official will have to call it and everyone will say he caused the player to foul.

Question: What is and is not pass interference?

Answer: Well, look at it this way—two players are running down the field, full bore, and they're both looking up at the ball. They're both making a simultaneous and bona fide attempt to go for the ball and their feet tangle up and you don't see a flag for a call. Everybody in the stands moans and groans and says what the hell is the matter with those dumbbells out there? Didn't they see it? Don't they know what pass interference is? You bet they do. The problem is that the guy in the stands doesn't know what it is. He'd like a call to be made in favor of his team but that's not how it's done.

The rule states that once the ball is in the air, and each player is playing the ball and not the other man, there is no pass interference. This does not mean that a player can come up on another player and go "right through him" trying to get to the ball.

Here is a play that had the TV commentators second-guessing the officials during the 1977 season.

One of the fastest men in football, a receiver, was on a straight downfield pattern. It was obvious he would beat the defensive back. So, the defensive back got in front of him, looked back over his shoulder at the ball, and slowed down, causing the swift receiver to run into his back, and they both hit the turf.

Question: Do officials apologize to players when they have made a mistaken call?

Answer: If it's correctable the official would correct it. If not, I usually said, "I'll be checking the same films as you and if I blew it, I'm sorry. But, there's nothing we can do about it now so let's play ball."

Question: What call do officials miss the most?

Answer: When a receiver catches a pass two or three yards inbounds and is hit and driven backwards and out of bounds. Inexperienced officials will usually mark the spot where the receiver went out of bounds, instead of where he was hit, (i.e. if the catch is on the forty and the receiver is driven out on the thirty-seven, the next down should start on the forty.) This becomes especially crucial if the spot to be gained for a first down is between the thirty-seven and the forty.

Question: How many eligible pass receivers are there?

Answer: Most people think there are five, the two ends and the three backs. The quarterback is not eligible. But, there are eleven men on the defense who are also eligible. All sixteen of these men have protection under the pass interference rules.

Question: I've seen you guys on television in lousy, freezing weather. How do you keep from freezing to death?

Answer: The first layer is a pair of lightweight long johns. The next is a pair of thermal long johns. If it's really cold you then cut arm and head holes in a plastic suit bag and slip that over the long johns. Then comes a turtleneck dickey, followed by the striped shirt and white knickers.

Most of us carry a knit skier's headband to protect our ears, and rely upon the white cap to protect our head. All this is great, but unless you protect your feet, you die.

Next to your skin you wear long white cotton stockings. Then you take a plastic tube that the baker uses to package French bread and pull it over the stockings. You squeeze the air out of it and tape it around your ankles. Then comes the sweat socks, the saddle stockings with the white stripes and the shoes. The shoes and the sweat socks will get soaking wet and freezing cold, but your feet are sweating inside the plastic bag. Some officials wear gloves. I never could, because I had to handle the ball on every play. A couple of days later, a friend says to you, "I saw you on TV Sunday, and you're sure gaining weight."

Question: Do the NFL crews stay together for the whole season?

Answer: In the preseason games they mix the crews, but once the regular season starts the crews stay together for the rest of the season.

Question: How much does the NFL pay their officials?

Answer: The NFL pays their officials according to seniority. The pay scale as of this writing follows. However, negotiations were under way to press time and there will be a higher scale starting with the 1978 season.

OFFICIALS' COMPENSATION

1. Preseason game fee. . . . . $300 per game

2. Regular season game fee plan:

    a.) 1st and 2nd year men. . . . . $325 per game
    b.) 3rd and 4th year men. . . . . $375 per game
    c.) 5th and 6th year men . . . . $425 per game
    d.) 7th and 8th year men. . . . . $475 per game
    e.) 9th and 10th year men . . . . $525 per game
    f.) 11 year men and beyond . . . . $575 per game

Officials working night games other than Friday or Saturday receive an additional $100.

3. Postseason game fees:

Super Bowl. $1,500
Super Bowl Alternate . . . . $ 700
American Conference Championship $1,000
National Conference Championship. $1,000
Divisional Play-offs $1,000
Alternate on above three . . . . $ 500
NFL All-Star Game . . . . $ 700
All-Star Game Alternate. $ 350

4. The flat rate game expense is $60. If a league night game is involved which requires two nights' lodging, a maximum of $95 is allowed.

5. The league pays for first class air travel on all assignments.

Question: What do you think of the suggestion that the NFL should have full-time officials?

Answer: Each season when divisional titles become tight, some of the people who disagree with an official's call will say that the NFL needs full-time officials. One coach was quoted in the newspapers as saying that there were lots of guys walking the streets who would be glad to be a full-time official for $17,500 a year.

He probably doesn't understand where the NFL officials come from. Just like the players, they are extensively scouted and selected from the very best officials working major college football. Because college football is played only once a week, about twelve weeks a year, it is impossible for a man to make a living as a football official. He has to have an off-the-field, full-time job. The men who reach the pinnacle of big time college ball are also highly successful in their occupations of medicine, law, business and education.

There is no way they could afford to take the large cut in their present incomes necessary to work for $17,500 a year as a full-time official. I agree, though, with the coach. There are plenty of men who would like to do the job for $17,500, but very few of them could meet the present stringent requirements for NFL officials.

The fact that these men are highly successful in their business and professions is an added plus to the league. They have been used to public and crucial challenges. They are men who have records of pressure applied, and pressure withstood. They have attained high levels of success and are determined to keep that capacity high during their football assignments on the weekend.

Officials at the NFL level are not interested in having a union represent them. They don't intend for their Sunday jobs to become their full-time occupations. They know that the best things they can do to keep them in shape for their Sunday business is to constantly look for new ways to improve themselves during the week, in their work of making decisions in medicine, law, education and business. A majority of officials are management oriented. Many times during Professional Referees Association meetings, I have heard someone say, "I'll pay the expenses for one of us to go to New York to talk to the commissioner and owners, but I'll quit before I'll let some attorney or union organizer talk for me."

But, if officiating becomes a full-time job, I am afraid an officials' union, like the ones in baseball and basketball, is soon to come. It makes me shudder to think what will happen if the NFL should turn its game over to a group of inexpensive full-time officials. However, if the salary is raised to forty or fifty thousand dollars a year, then they might be able to attract some of the top officiating talent. And, if they're lucky, they'll get the same guys they have now.

SEVENTEEN

I don't know if you have heard about the university that sent psychological questionnaires to one hundred of the top refs in the country. Did you get one, John?

Yes. I see that John raised his hand. Well, folks. One thing they found out was that ninety percent of the refs were bottle babies. You see, John, even your own mother wouldn't trust you.

Joe Paterno, Head Football Coach
Penn State University
First Friday Friars Luncheon

So now you want to be an official. You've decided that you'd rather be on the field during the game, yet not in all the pushing and shoving and running around? Well, all right!

All NFL officials must have a minimum of ten years' experience in officiating football, five of which have been on the varsity collegiate or minor professional level. You have to belong to an officials' association and have previous experience as a player or coach. Officials for the most part are take-charge people, yet not overpowering. They are strong in the areas of self-confidence and the capacity to influence others. The self-confidence is a necessity in order to disregard the thunderous jeers of an angry crowd.

If you're still interested, call a local high school coach or

athletic director. Ask him to give you the name of a secretary or commissioner of an officials' association. When you become a member of an officials' organization they will help you learn the language and mechanics of the trade.

Your first assignments will probably be at the lower high school level. Take them. Don't get upset because you weren't given a varsity game immediately. And get used to the mistakes the kids will be making. Most important though, is for you to have patience living through your own mistakes and the awkward situations in which you'll find yourself. Be easy on yourself but don't start believing, after a few good calls, that you're now ready for a college or pro game. You're not.

Expand your sensitivities to all elements of the game, but

remember, you're not out there to befriend anybody. Don't give anyone any kind of sympathy because their team isn't doing well, but try to understand the total situation. Remember, the coaches have their livelihoods in the hands of a group of fifteen- and sixteen-year-old kids.

Before each game you may want to go up to each head coach and ask if they are planning to run anything "that premature judgment on our part might spoil."

If you're the referee, always deal with the team captains to discuss fouls, time-outs, overall team control and player cooperation. In pregame conferences with captains tell them that you expect their total support in maintaining game control. If any player gives anybody a bad time you always have the option of going to the captain to help you straighten his player out. This is particularly a good idea when players want to argue with you.

In pro ranks the captains are the same for every game of the season. This helps officiating because we get used to working with them during the game. These men are good to work with because they are usually people who maintain poise in stressful situations. They are also some of the most respected players on the squad. Each year the NFL sends us a list of the teams and their captains.

In a Denver game, a rookie player started arguing with me after I called him for holding. His captain, Bud McFadin, came over and pushed him back and told him, "You've got enough trouble playing your own position so don't start telling him how to do his job."

Let the captain take charge of his team and you've got the battle half won.

If a captain asks you what he should do when you give him his options after a foul is called, tell him, "The same thing you'll do as soon as you make up your mind." It works every time.

The last regular season NFL game I worked was in a snowstorm in Connecticut between the Giants and the Vikings, on December 5, 1973. I called for a measurement in the game with about eight seconds remaining. One of the defensive players on the Vikings called out to me, "Oh, come on, John, give it to 'em. Get the thing over with. We're freezing out here."

The score was clear out of sight, but I had to measure. I had to know. Did they make it or not. They did, and after one more play the game was over. But the measurement was necessary. We had to call for the chain to measure. You work the last minute of a game just like you work the first one.

After a game is over get off the field as fast as you can. Don't stand around waiting to solicit questions from anyone. You'll get into a lot more trouble with your mouth than you will with your flag.

When you make a call, report it to the referee and then, if you can, go to the coach and tell him, "Number 65, holding." *That's all you need to tell him.* If he objects to the call you made, anything you do to explain it will often be interpreted by him as you trying to make excuses for any mistakes he thought you made during the game. If he comes up to you after the game and wants to know about a ruling, you can give him an explanation. After the explanation, he may moan about the call. Don't be apologetic. "That's how we saw it," is all you can say. No sorrowful speeches are required.

After you've worked high school games for a few years you'll want to apply to junior college and four-year college leagues. Be careful. When they ask for recommendations don't send them letters from your friends, telling what a great guy you are. Letters about your officiating ability should come from those people who know you best in this area—assignment secretaries, commissioners, or veteran officials. Unless requested, do not send letters from coaches.

Character references may be required. Only send the letters they ask for. No league that I know of wants to be deluged with unsolicited letters. I would see to it that an official in the league to which you're applying has seen you at work. Each year the NFL selects a few men from hundreds of applicants for observation. These men have successfully passed through a number of screening processes, and have reached the point where the league wants to see them work a four-year college game. The league sends their own observers to do the evaluation because they don't want anything other than the official's performance to influence their decision.

When I was hiring officials for the WFL, one applicant sent me fifty-three letters from coaches who recommended him. All that did was convince me that he spent much of his time, especially before and after each game, trying to get coaches to like him. We didn't ask for fifty-three, we asked for six. I got one application from a man who had no officiating experience at all. He said he had talked with NFL officials a few times and that he was sure that he could handle calling a pro game. He hadn't learned the rule book, hadn't taken any of the complicated set of officials' tests, learned the mechanics, or blown one game whistle.

In evaluating an official's work, the most important element is the mechanics—the officials' positioning and movement on the field.

Was he at the right place at the right time to cover the play? Did he make the call with authority? Did he "sell" the call? He doesn't have to make a big show when he makes a call, but he has to move quickly and with authority.

Did he go to the spot that is necessary for the call to be made? Did he go to the referee immediately to tell him about the foul? On a potential pass play, did he stand deep enough, or was he too deep downfield? Observers of officials will want to know if a flanking official covers his sideline well enough, and does he turn when he is supposed to. If the official is the referee, does he stand and watch the ball go through the air, or is he intent on watching what is happening to the quarterback, and the people who are coming after him?

Suppose it's late in the game and the team with the ball is behind. They're not going to sit on the ball or try to grind out yardage up the middle. An official has got to be ready for the quick shots to the outside. Shots where a guy is going to catch the ball and step out of bounds to kill the clock. You're going to be out there anticipating his stepping out, and be ready to signal to stop the clock, the instant his foot hits the sidelines. You've got to be ready with the signal. It's got to be instinctive.

The pros are masters at conserving and consuming time. A Namath, a Griese, a Stabler can control a game with their use of time. They'll throw the ball and whirl around and tell you "time-out" the instant the ball is caught. Sometime they'll call time-out before the ball is caught, but you, the ref, will have to make them wait until the ball becomes dead downfield before you can make the official signal. I worked with some quarterbacks who would tell me before a play to call time-out as soon as their end was tackled with the caught ball, or stepped out of bounds after a completion. They knew better than to expect that type of service from me but still they tried.

A good official communicates through body language that he is confident about his mechanics. Sitting in the stands I can't tell how well he knows his rules, but I will know if he working his mechanics correctly. If an official keeps patting his head to signal for an ineligible receiver downfield—oversignalling. If he looks unsure of himself when he runs to the referee, and if he isn't direct and deliberate with his motions, then he's not going to make it to the higher levels of competition.

I am always fascinated at the shock former players and coaches have when we tell them they have to start officiating at the freshman and junior varsity high school level. Especially when they felt they should have started as college officials. I lost count of the former coaches who came to me after the first two or three clinics and said, "If I had taken this clinic before I started to coach I would have been a hundred times better coach."

The worn out theory, "good player, good coach, good official," just doesn't hold up in actual practice. Each element of the game takes special skills that must be learned, practiced, and internalized until they become a part of you, naturally.

There is no question in my mind that every coach would do himself, his team, and his overall coaching program a tremendous amount of good by becoming an official in some sport. By getting a feel for how the men in the striped shirts see and work the game, he will improve his own communications with the officials who work his games.

Officials have to be there, no matter what—colds, backaches, headaches, or whatever else is temporarily ailing—you have to show. There are no standbys.

If you sprain an ankle, twist an arm, or break a nose in a game, most likely you'll be back in the game, one or two plays later. Paul Lowe, who played for the Chargers and the Chiefs, asked me in the middle of a game, "Hey, I was just thinking about it. You guys don't have time to sit down, do you?"

"No, we're just a bunch of old men out here. You guys do all of the hitting and shoving and we do most of the running. (Officials run close to seven or eight miles a game.)

The only games that have standby officials are the playoffs. In a regular season game, if an official should get seriously hurt, the crew would use officiating mechanics designed for one less man. One Monday night, an official was injured and carried out of the game. Another official, who wasn't working that day, but lived in the game city, was called to finish the game. The announcers called him the alternate official, but actually, he was a lives-nearby official.

I was in a game in Oakland once, trying to get out of the way of a scrambling quarterback, when my left calf knotted up. On the next play I was hobbling around, trying to stay out of his way when my other calf knotted up.

With all toes pointed in and both calves knotted, I could barely walk to the bench. When I got there all of the players gave me a bad time. Some suggested that I go to preseason camp with them to *really* get in shape. A few plays later I tried to get back in the game, but I couldn't make it. When I returned to the bench I was greeted by hooting cheers. The players had one less policeman out there to hide from.

One of the easiest ways to stay on the bench and work your way out of the league, is to eat your way out. No league wants their officials to become obese. It's not easy for the people in the league office to defend an official when the first thing an irate coach or owner says when he complains, is that, "He's so fat and out of shape, no wonder he can't keep up with the action."

My nose was broken or smashed six times as an official. I think that's a record, at least for noses broken in the same direction (right to left). The last time was when I caught the tip of Dick Butkus' shoulder pads. Dick was not only a tough linebacker. He had tough shoulder pads.

The best public relations for officials when they are off the field is to have no public relations. There is no need for you to be going around broadcasting that you will be officiating the game tomorrow afternoon.

Leagues are quite interested in knowing the people with whom you associate. Early in the AFL, we were working a game in Dallas. The night before a game, Clyde Devine, our umpire, went down to the main dining room in our hotel to make reservations for the early dinner show. We had been told that the reservations were sold out. When he came back he told us, "The guy said he didn't have a table for us right now, but I am sure he will. I gave him half of this." He showed us the kept half of a ten-dollar bill.

In about twenty minutes the phone rang and the restaurant captain had a table for us. The next morning we got a call from our supervisor who was in Buffalo, New York. He had received a report from the league's security detail that one of the men on our crew was seen giving money to a known gambler. The other half of that ten-dollar bill was given to a man who was once a bookie in New York City. Everything possible is done to make sure that the score on the scoreboard is strictly determined by the playing of the players on the field. We don't mind the close scrutiny and, we don't mind the first class way we travel to and from games. We're also paid very well.

Pro officials belong to an organization called the Professional Referees' Association. It got the name, Referees' Association, instead of Officials' Association because the attorney who drew up the incorporation papers thought that we were all called referees. So we just let the name stand, to the chagrin of some of the linesmen, umpires, et al. It's not a union, and most of the officials would object if it were.

The association sends a group of officials to New York after each season to meet with league executives. One of the finest things those meetings have produced is a pension plan for officials. The officials who represented us in the negotiations were Ed Marion, Ben Drieth, Bill O'Brien, George Ellis and Jim Tunney. The agreement stipulated that any man who had ten years or more of service in the league would receive two hundred and fifty dollars per month when he reaches the age of sixty-five. The starting point was set for those who were on the active roster for the 1974 season. Ten of us barely missed that date because we retired in 1973. Our organization asked the owners if the plan could go back a few years to pick us up, but they felt that the plan originally agreed to was fair enough.

The officials then took action at their next annual meeting to increase the amount of annual dues paid to the association, so that the ten of us who retired in 1973 would be included with the same kind of pension that will be awarded to the later retirees. That's some of the greatest togetherness ever demonstrated off the field.

I would like to see the association take on a project of

getting recognition for members of the third team on the field in the Professional Football Hall of Fame. I will even go so far as to nominate some men for the first group of official inductees—Ron Gibbs, "Dutch" Heinz, Dan Tehan, Bud Brubaker, "Red" Pace, and Norm Schachter.

If you decide to become an on-the-field or in-the-stands official I hope your time behind the whistle gives you as much satisfaction and thrills my thirty years of striped shirt service have given me. If the day ever comes that players start admitting and calling their own fouls and start walking off yardage against their own teams, the whistle will become obsolete. Then all the "used to be" officials will take their place in the stands with the rest of the world and the game, with all its pain and beauty, can be played forever.

BOOKS OF RELATED INTEREST

THE RUNNING SAGA OF WALTER STACK by Bob Bishop is the incredible true story of a 71-year-old marathon runner who began running at age 57 and has run over 70 marathons (26 miles, 385 yards each). His daily schedule would defeat a man half his age and his life-style would never make the family hour on TV but his love of people and life is contagious.
160 pages, soft cover, $4.95

SOCCER by Jack Grant (author of the best-selling SKATEBOARD-ING) is a guide for players, coaches and parents on the physical, social and emotional aspects of the game. Grant draws on his 15 years as player and coach to provide a team and an individual perspective of the sport.
192 pages, soft cover, $5.95

RUNNING HOME by Michael Spino is a comprehensive six-week fitness program including fully illustrated instructions for running, breathing, stretching and yoga postures. Nutrition, methods of measuring progress, and how to organize a permanent program are discussed.
160 pages, soft cover, $5.95

BEYOND JOGGING by Michael Spino contains all you will ever need to know to develop a jogging program. The book brings together spiritual concepts such as meditation and body aware-ness with the physical techniques, making jogging a creative experience.
128 pages, soft cover, $3.95

PLAYING TENNIS WHEN IT HURTS by K. Gordon Campbell M.D., a tennis playing orthopedist, gives detailed instructions on playing without aggravating an injury, preventing injuries, over-coming and healing injuries while continuing to play, and how to warm up properly.
112 pages, soft cover, $4.95

Available at your local book or department store or directly from the publisher. To order by mail, send check or money order to:

CELESTIAL ARTS
231 Adrian Road
Millbrae, California 94030

Please include $1.00 for postage and handling. California residents add 6% tax.